I saw him once and heard him speak. It was at the first international convention of the Brotherhood of St. Andrew, at Buffalo, N.Y. October, 1897

Wm. T. Orne
Jan. 97

March, 1940

Bishop
Whipple's
SOUTHERN
DIARY
1843–1844

Bishop Whipple's SOUTHERN DIARY

1843–1844

EDITED WITH
AN INTRODUCTION BY

LESTER B. SHIPPEE

LONDON · HUMPHREY MILFORD · OXFORD UNIVERSITY PRESS

THE UNIVERSITY OF MINNESOTA PRESS
Minneapolis

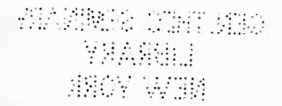

CONTENTS

LIST OF ILLUSTRATIONS

Introduction

HENRY BENJAMIN WHIPPLE

The journal kept by Henry Benjamin Whipple and reproduced in this little volume is copied from a blank book in
which entries were made by the young man during the latter
part of 1843 and the early months of 1844 while he traveled
through Florida, Georgia, Mississippi, Louisiana, and then up
the Mississippi as far as St. Louis, down to the Ohio, up that
river, and then overland through the states of Ohio, Pennsylvania, Delaware, Virginia, and Maryland. In general the
record speaks for itself. While unquestionably intended to be
read by others than himself, it is characterized by a frankness
and freedom of comment which make it a valuable first-hand
account of the social phenomena with which he was brought
in contact. The acuteness of observation, the ability to describe what he saw as well as to analyze impressions of people
and things foreshadowed qualities that marked his later life.

Such a record would be of importance had it been left by
one who never afterward made himself conspicuous in any
way, but coming from a man whose later life was of so much
significance in his state, in the nation, and, indeed, in the
world at large, this diary becomes doubly interesting. A gen-

eration ago the name of Bishop Whipple was known and
revered in a wide circle in the United States and abroad. His
pioneer episcopate in a frontier state, his part in the development of Minnesota for nearly half a century, his contributions
to the establishment of its education, and above all his unflag-
ging zeal in trying to obtain something like justice for the
Indians identified him in a manner almost spectacular with
the social development of the United States during the dec-
ades between the opening of the Civil War and the close of
the nineteenth century.

The future Bishop of Minnesota was born in Adams, Jefferson County, New York, on February 15, 1822. His father,
John Hall Whipple, was a representative of transplanted
New England stock in upstate New York—a Rhode Islander
one generation removed, whose father had broken the bonds
which had kept four generations of Whipples in Cumberland, where the firstcomer had purchased land from one of
the original white occupants. His mother was Elizabeth
Wager, daughter of another New York pioneer. Devout
Presbyterians, his parents had their son educated in local
schools of that denomination, intending that he should pro-
ceed by way of a college training to some profession. Frail
health, however, thwarted these plans, although young
Whipple did spend a year (1838–39) at Oberlin Institute,
where an uncle was a member of the faculty.

At this radical Western institution he encountered doctrines which appear to have raised disturbing thoughts in the
young man's mind, as we may gather from a letter written
him by a maternal uncle at Utica: "I hope you will return to
Oberlin with cheerfulness, if it be the desire of your parents
that you should do so. For I have not the least fear that you
will become a fanatic, though you may be surrounded by

them. You appear to take a rational view of abolitionism and are as I am glad to see, what every true friend of American freedom is, a rational abolitionist."

Five years later Whipple, in his journal, gave evidence that he was still a "rational abolitionist." He had not been converted to the extreme views of the Oberlin school. Indeed, for a young fellow who had barely reached his majority at a time when slavery was beginning to be a burning issue, he exhibited a surprising saneness and objectivity in his comments on the "peculiar institution," comments which one might more reasonably expect from an intelligent citizen of a border state than from a New Yorker of New England extraction who had come under the influence of abolitionists of the Western Reserve.

Uncertain health put an end to Whipple's formal education, and he joined his father in the latter's business. In October, 1842, he married Cornelia, daughter of a fellow townsman, Benjamin Wright, and seemed about to settle down to a lifetime in Adams. Hardly a year had passed, however, before he was forced to take drastic measures to recuperate his frail physique, and then came the enforced winter vacation in the South and the journal which he kept during his absence from home. The journal does not wholly indicate the hold which the South and particularly Florida obtained upon its writer. Ten years later (1853–54), when Mrs. Whipple's health was delicate, both of them spent several months in the very region which had been so graphically described on the occasion of his first visit, and in his later years Bishop Whipple was accustomed to pass part of the winter season there in order to escape the rigors of Minnesota's climate.

Until 1848 business and a lively interest in politics, an interest which crops up in the journal rather frequently, occupied the young man. His political bent may well be told in his own words:

From earliest youth I had been deeply interested in political affairs, and had tried to follow the teachings of the founders of the Republic. I felt that if good men were to be nominated for office, good men must attend the primary meetings. My influence was beyond my years, for I believed in the lessons of my saintly mother, "never hesitate to defend the weak and never be afraid if God is on your side." My father belonged to the old Whig party, but he was one of those broad-minded men who would never interfere with the conscientious convictions of others. I became a Democrat of the conservative school. Through the influence of Governor Dix I was appointed by Governor Marcy, Division Inspector with the rank of Colonel, on the staff of Major-General Corse, having been previously appointed Major by Governor William L. Bouck. It afforded many pleasant hours of recreation with the fuss and feathers of military equipage. During the scare of the Patriot rebellion in Canada we were ordered to the defence of the frontier, but the Government wisely sent some regulars who settled the matter before we entered upon actual service, and our military reputations were saved. My last service in the political field was as secretary of a state convention.

Thurlow Weed and Edwin Croswell, two of New York's political leaders, said when I became a candidate for Holy Orders that they "hoped a good politician had not been spoiled to make a poor preacher." Many of these political friends became my helpers in my struggles to secure justice for the Indians. Governor Seymour, General John A. Dix, and others, never failed to give me their influence with the authorities at Washington.[1]

Testimony to support the conviction that Whipple was no mere armchair politician is found in a letter written him in the autumn of 1846 by O. Hungerford, who told him that he was to be relied upon to do the campaign work in Rodman and Henderson.

[1] *Lights and Shadows of a Long Episcopate* (3d printing, New York, 1902), pp. 5–6.

*Henry Benjamin Whipple and his
daughter Jane, about 1849*

But business and politics both began to take a secondary place as Whipple grew more and more convinced that his life work lay in the Christian ministry. Unquestionably the influence of Mrs. Whipple was a determining factor in his decision to turn from his Presbyterian upbringing to the Protestant Episcopal Church and to prepare himself for Holy Orders; furthermore, his grandparents had been Episcopalians. He began preparation for his new vocation in March, 1848; in August, 1849, he was ordained deacon and the next year he became a priest. For seven years, with the exception of the months he spent in Florida, he was rector of Zion Church in Rome, New York. During this time he received a number of calls from other places: "I received calls from Grace Church, Chicago, St. Paul's Church, Milwaukee, to Terre Haute, and several other places; but I loved my flock and they loved me and, as there was every sign that God's blessing rested on my work, I declined all calls."[2]

There did come, however, a call which struck a responsive chord in the young priest's heart. Albert F. Neely of Chicago appealed to him to take up work among railroad men, clerks, and laborers in a section of Chicago where no church had yet been established, and from this appeal came his determination to leave Zion Church, Rome, and go to the Free Church of the Holy Communion, which had been organized by a handful of men to make it possible to call Whipple. This was in 1857. With no misgivings in his own mind, but accompanied by dire forebodings from his friends and relatives, Whipple left the established things of his youth and turned to the new field in the "wild West." He labored successfully for two years, making for himself a respected position among men of a type far removed from that with which he had

[2] *Lights and Shadows*, p. 18.

grown up. It was his success in this Chicago field, which was not far removed from missionary endeavor, that brought him to the attention of others and led to his nomination as Bishop of Minnesota in 1859.

Here was a real missionary opportunity. Minnesota, it was true, had grown enough in population to have just been admitted to the Union as a state, but the frontier fringe was still close to the Mississippi, and St. Paul, Minneapolis, and St. Anthony were only crude frontier towns. Whipple's nomination was confirmed by the General Convention, and in October, 1859, he was consecrated at Richmond, Virginia, by Bishop de Lancy, who had ordained him both deacon and priest. In November he held his first service in his new diocese at Wabasha. Against the advice of the secretary of the Board of Missions he chose Faribault for his residence:

My reasons regarding the opposition were that it [Faribault] was the only place in the state which had offered me definite pledges for a residence; it gave me the hope of meeting my expenses without debt; it was the centre of a rapidly growing section of Minnesota, and it offered me the prospect for the establishment of Church schools.[3]

It was here, in the southern part of the state, not far from the Iowa border, that the cornerstone of the Bishop's Church was laid in July, 1862; it was here that, largely as a result of Bishop Whipple's energies, a notable group of educational institutions was established: Seabury Divinity School, St. Mary's School for Girls, and Shattuck Military Academy, as well as the Wilder School for young farmers. The bishop had a persuasive way with people, and he accumulated, not without difficulty but successfully, the money necessary to establish and operate these institutions, and that at a time when war, Indian troubles, and the hardships of economic depression in

[3] *Lights and Shadows,* pp. 59–60.

a new state made every kind of philanthropic endeavor very discouraging.

A frontier missionary, whether bishop or humble worker in the field, had no easy time. Salaries, if they can be so dignified, were small and hard to get. Moreover, in addition to his other difficulties Bishop Whipple was plagued by the obligations which fell upon him when his father died. Early in 1861, responding to a call for financial assistance, he wrote that his expenses were heavy and "it would be a happy day if I could pay every debt of my poor dead father—debts in no way having the least shadow of claim upon me, which I never heard of till his death. When at Adams we left everything and brought away my widowed and penniless mother." To another he wrote: "My poor father's estate, unable to satisfy a fourth of claims, mother destitute, the whole family poor, an uncle turned oppressor to deny our rights and urge an old claim on which I was an endorser."

Two distinct lines of activity engaged Whipple's attention as bishop: his duty toward his white flock and attention to the needs of the Indians. It is apparent that at times some complaint was voiced about his zeal in behalf of his red brethren, for, in April, 1861, he felt called upon to notice it in a letter to an Eastern correspondent: "I have been accused of neglecting my white field & wasting money on Indian missions. I have since last June preached over two hundred sermons to white men. I have preached probably thirty times to Indians since my consecration." The whole of the Sioux outfit for six months with three men in the field, he added, was but $445 and the Chippewa mission for a year was less than a thousand dollars, in spite of the fact that one of the laborers supplied two stations more than twenty miles apart.

Hardly had the new bishop become settled in his diocese

when the sectional conflict which had been looming on the horizon broke into the war between the states. On this issue he had no question in his mind as to the principles involved. To a correspondent, probably his brother-in-law, he wrote in July, 1861:

Your strictures upon my course are very natural for one whose views favor secession. Whether just or not they are conscientiously given. I see nothing in it but anarchy and ruin. Yet never did I feel more kindly disposed towards the south. My position is that of thousands of churchmen at the north. We love you as brethren, and are ready to prove our love by gladly conceding to you all a Christian has the right to yield for peace. You shall have every guarantee of the Constitution and if we have wronged you a hair's breadth we will take it back before the world. But as between this love and duty to the best government on earth, duty to relations where the Catholic church has advantages to spread the gospel she has not had for 1500 years, we must stand by the country if it costs everything.

Called upon to be chaplain of the First Minnesota Volunteers, Whipple was forced to decline because he felt that his work at home had a stronger demand upon his services. He did, however, preach to the regiment at Fort Snelling in May, just before the unit left for service, and was with it again after the Battle of Antietam, where it had been in the hottest part of the fray. Two other times during the course of the war the Bishop was in Washington, primarily to plead the cause of the Indians, and on each occasion he visited the army and held services.

Whatever may be the topic one takes up in considering the career of Bishop Whipple, the Indians are sure to appear. Had there been no Indian problem, his work would still have left for him the reputation of an outstanding personality, yet it is his indefatigable labors for the red man for which he is best known. An Episcopal mission among the Chippewa had been established as early as 1852 at Gull Lake. Before he had been in his diocese a month Whipple visited this place in the company of the Reverend J. L. Breck. The hunger, squalor, and generally miserable situation of these aborigines stirred the bishop's heart, which "insensibly . . . was touched and prepared for the love which I was to feel for this poor people." It did not take him long to discover that their misery had been caused largely by their contact with the whites; the rapacity of the whites, the venality and incompetence of the Indian agents, had spelled ruin in the past and promised nothing better for the future. Letter after letter written in these early days of his episcopate dwells upon the subject and upon the need for a thoroughgoing revision of the whole governmental Indian policy. The gist of his strictures is well summed up in the plea he made to President Lincoln early in 1862:[4]

The Indian agents who are placed in trust of the honor and faith of the Government are generally selected without any reference to the fitness for the place. The congressional delegations desire to reward John Doe for party work, and John Doe desires the place because there is a tradition on the border that an Indian agent with fifteen hundred dollars a year can retire upon an ample fortune in four years.

The Indian agent appoints his subordinates from the same motive either to reward his friends' service or to fulfil the bidding of his congressional patron. They are often men without any fitness, sometimes a disgrace to a Christian nation, whiskey sellers, bar room loungers, debauchees selected to guide a heathen people. Then follow all the evils of bad example of inefficiency and of dishonesty. The school a show, the supplies wasted, the improvement fund squandered by negligence or curtailed by fraudulent contracts. The Indian bewildered, conscious of wrong but helpless, has no refuge but to sink into a depth of brutishness never known to his fathers. . . .

[4] The letter bears no date, but was written late in February or early in March.

The United States has virtually left the Indian without protection. Thefts, murders and rapes are common and no one pays more attention to them than if they were swine. I can count up more than a dozen murders which have taken place in the Chippewa country within two years past. I have heard of a woman violated by a party of white devils where death ensued but there was no law to protect the innocent or punish the guilty.

The sale of whiskey, the open licentiousness, the neglect and want is fast dooming this people to death and as sure as there is a God much of the guilt lies at the nation's door.

The Indians, Whipple contended, could become civilized. There was, however, need of a program that would include (1) honest agents, (2) instructions to treat them as wards of the Government, (3) permission, if the Indian wished, to abandon his wild life and settle upon an open farm where he would be supplied with a house, proper utensils, and tools, (4) schools which would receive all who desired to attend, (5) future treaties securing to the Indians payments in kind and not in money, and (6) a concentration of scattered Chippewa on a single reservation where the United States agent should be empowered to try all violations of Indian laws.

A few days later (March 6) the bishop again appealed to the President:

I would not add a feather's weight to the heavy burden of your heart, but I plead to some one for my poor heathen wards who have no one else to plead for them. Where shall a Christian Bishop look for justice if not to you whom God has made the chief Ruler of the nation.

I wrote to your predecessor and no notice was taken of it. Will you not take a half hour to read my plea and so instruct the department that something may be done to a people whose cry calls for the vengeance of God.

Not only to the President, who acknowledged receipt of Whipple's appeal in a way that gave him hope that something would be done, were letters addressed on the plight of the Indians, but to Caleb B. Smith, secretary of the interior, to Senator Morton L. Wilkinson, to Cyrus Aldrich, and to Senator Rice, who was asked to call upon the President to urge him to indorse a proposal for the appointment of a commission to work out some comprehensive scheme of action.

Presently an event took place that gave tragic point to the picture Whipple had spread before the President. On the morning of August 18, 1862, a band of Dakota attacked a village of traders and their employees in the Minnesota Valley and opened the famous Sioux Outbreak which kept the state in a turmoil for months. Goaded to exasperation by hunger, due in part to the delay in receiving their annual payments, by their grievances against the whites, particularly the traders who had cheated them for years, and by the general belief that the Government, which had promised them protection when treaties were made, had forgotten them, the Sioux spread fire and slaughter along a wide line of the Minnesota frontier. Their gesture was futile, for, as some of the friendly Indians had tried to tell their less patient fellows, they stood no chance against the whites. On the contrary, the outbreak occasioned a demand not only for the punishment of all participants in the attack but for the removal of all Indians from the whole region.

To meet and counteract this overwhelming demand for wholesale and indiscriminate executions, Bishop Whipple set himself the task of changing public opinion by appeals through the press and appeals to the President. In the hot wrath which possessed the people of the state they were quick to charge him with being a supporter of the Indians against the whites. Among them were some upon whom he had felt that he could count to uphold his plea for sanity and moderation. Senator Rice seemed to think that he was trying to protect murderers, and General Sibley that his desire to have justice tempered with mercy was being carried to the point of maudlin sentimentality. Governor Ramsey, General Pope, and the greater portion of the press insisted upon exemplary punishment, failing which the people of Minnesota, they said, would take the case into their own hands. Whipple was in Washington in the autumn. Accompanied by General Halleck, his cousin, he called upon President Lincoln, to whom he gave an account of the Indian situation and urged not only moderation in taking revenge but formulation of a policy that would prevent such outbreaks in the future. This counsel undoubtedly had some effect, for the President commuted the sentences of or pardoned all but thirty-nine of the accused, and instead of hanging three hundred the people of Minnesota had to be content with the execution of this smaller number.[5]

Despite Bishop Whipple's efforts to save their lands, at least for those Sioux who had not participated in the outbreak, popular demand for their removal from Minnesota was so insistent that Congress, by act of March, 1863, made provision for transferring them elsewhere. The act was one of supererogation, for by the time General Sibley's campaign against the Upper Sioux was completed, only fragmentary bands were wandering in Dakota Territory, where, by the Treaty of 1867, they were eventually settled upon two reservations.

Only the Chippewa were now left in Minnesota and over them Whipple watched until 1895, when his diocese was

[5] For an account of the Sioux Outbreak see William W. Folwell, *A History of Minnesota* (St. Paul, 1921–30), 2:109–301.

divided and the Indians were committed to the spiritual care of the Bishop of Duluth. In 1864 his plea in Washington obtained for the Red Lake band a treaty which had some semblance of equity, especially if compared with one made the year before. In 1886 he was a member of the Northwest Indian Commission, which was appointed largely as a result of his representations to President Cleveland, and which attempted to concentrate all the Minnesota Chippewa on the White Earth Reservation. In short, between his long journeys to visit his wards and his trips to Washington, one wonders how he found time for the many other tasks in his diocese.

While it cannot be said that the United States government has even yet evolved a satisfactory Indian policy, the agitation of Bishop Whipple and like-minded persons did produce some results, particularly in the administrations of Presidents Grant and Cleveland. In 1870 was brought to an end the policy of making treaties with Indian tribes as though they stood on equality with the United States; in that year there was a general appropriation for education, and in 1873 the more general "civilization fund" was abandoned. In 1887 the Dawes Act incorporated something of what Whipple had long sought—provision for individual allotments and ownership of land by Indians who could be naturalized as citizens of the United States. The Bishop saw at least some of the worst features of the system done away.

Probably no white man in Minnesota or in the whole Northwest had as much influence with individual Indians as did Bishop Whipple—"Straight Tongue" as his Indian name may be translated. He knew personally and followed the careers of scores, even hundreds, of individual Indians. They trusted him and went to him with their troubles. Like Elliott, he was truly an "Apostle to the Indians."

It was this work with the Indians that made him known outside his own state. Here and there scattered throughout the country were persons and groups who sought a better chance for the dispossessed Indian, and these looked to Whipple as a leader in the fight. They learned of his activities from the columns of religious journals, from the public press, and by word of mouth. His name became almost a household word. When, even as early as 1864–65, it was made possible for him to visit Europe for a vacation and rest, something of what he had done had gone before him, and he was widely acclaimed. Later, one may say, he was about as well known in England, at least by reputation, as in his own country. In 1871 he was offered the bishopric of the Sandwich Islands by the Archbishop of Canterbury but declined it because he felt that his work in Minnesota demanded all his energies and no foreign field could offer greater opportunities for service.

Many and varied were the evidences of his reputation. He received honorary degrees from Durham, Oxford, and Cambridge; he presided at bishops' meetings; in 1899 he represented the Protestant Episcopal Church of America at the London celebration of the centenary of the formation of the Missionary Society; he was the presiding bishop of the American Church at the third Pan-Anglican Conference in 1897; he was invited to preach in many if not most of the cathedrals of Great Britain. Tokens of appreciation, each preserving the memory of some place or some person who had done him honor, made the bishop's house in Faribault a veritable museum in Whipple's later years. Among these mementos was a signed portrait of Queen Victoria, who had heard from his own lips something of the work he had been doing.

With all his religious zeal and his philanthropic interests

Bishop Whipple in 1897

Whipple was no pedant or "holier-than-thou" type. He was equally at home in the Bishop's Palace at Durham and the logging camp of the frontier. He could meet all men on their own ground, whether they were railroad laborers in Chicago, Indians in their tepees, or pioneers in their log huts. Despite his never too robust physique he could and always did do his share of the work and bear his own burdens on the long journeys he was constantly making throughout his diocese. He tramped the trails with his guides and withstood the extremes of heat and cold of Minnesota seasons. Outdoor life had a great appeal for him. He was an ardent fisherman: the streams and lakes of Minnesota, the waters of Florida, the salmon runs of Scotland, all knew him. Among his papers is preserved a copy of the *Tarpon Record at Fort Myers, Florida, for the Season of 1892,* wherein it is stated that on March 3 Bishop Whipple caught a specimen which was six feet, seven inches long, weighing 124 pounds. Not the largest catch of that season but by no means the smallest.

Bishop Whipple had little time for literary composition, if one excepts his numerous sermons and occasional contributions to the press, both religious and secular. But he was a prolific letter writer and his list of correspondents was long and varied. It is no unusual thing to find in his letter books from a dozen to fifteen copies of letters written on the same day. Whether he had the desire to express himself in a more formal way there seems to be no means of determining, but if the desire was there, the time was lacking. Toward the end of his life, when his episcopal burdens had been lightened by the assistance of a coadjutor, he did consent to write and dictate some reminiscences. "Were it not," he said in the Preface, "for the many letters which come to me unceasingly from both sides of the Atlantic, asking for sketches of my diocesan and Indian work, I should hesitate to publish what must necessarily be a most unconventional and incomplete record of my work, owing to the brief time which I have been able to snatch from a crowded life. While, therefore, it has been impossible to give a detailed account of my connection with the Indians of the Northwest, I have given enough to enlighten those who are ignorant of the true state of Indian affairs, and to cause those more or less familiar with the facts to thank God for the light that is dawning." *Lights and Shadows of a Long Episcopate* appeared in 1899 and ran through three sizable printings. By this time Minnesotans had long since forgotten their exasperation over Whipple's stand on the Sioux troubles and looked upon him, along with Archbishop Ireland, as a citizen who reflected honor upon their state. They were proud of him and loved to bask in the reflected glory of his international reputation.

When, on September 16, 1901, he died at a ripe old age he was universally mourned. None grieved more deeply than his Indian friends, who flocked to Faribault to his funeral to express their sorrow and their appreciation of what he had done for their race. The young man who, almost sixty years before, had looked with an observant yet sympathetic eye upon a society which presented curious lights and shadows to a Northerner, had found a life work which brought out the best that was in him and had given full scope to a nature generous and understanding.

LESTER BURRELL SHIPPEE

October, 1937

EDITOR'S NOTE

This journal was found among Bishop Whipple's papers after his death and was deposited with the Minnesota Historical Society, St. Paul, in 1931. The entries were made in a large blank notebook from day to day. A few illustrations, mostly on letterheads, were pasted into the book. Three of these have been reproduced in the present edition. With the exception of the two portraits in the Introduction, the other illustrations are from contemporary sources.

In editing the manuscript for publication, such errors in spelling, capitalization, and punctuation have been corrected as are obviously slips of the pen such as inevitably occur in a hastily written, unrevised manuscript. Punctuation has been added where it would seem helpful to the reader. There has been no attempt, however, to introduce consistency into the punctuation, capitalization, and spelling, nor to make them conform to modern practice. Sentences similar in structure have not necessarily been punctuated the same; overcapitalization has not been modernized; many old-fashioned spellings have been left. Ease of reading has been the criterion followed throughout.

Bishop
Whipple's
SOUTHERN
DIARY
1843–1844

Through Georgia, Florida, Alabama, Louisiana, Mississippi River, Missouri, Ohio, Virginia, Maryland, Delaware, Pennsylvania

1843–1844

October 12th 1843. At the advice of my friend and physician I have today left my much loved home for a winter's residence at the south, in order if possible to recover my health. I believe all men feel sad at parting from home and how much more sad do those feel whose good fortune it is to have a home blessed with the presence of a loved wife and smiling babe. I felt as if, perhaps, this was my last farewell and I would no more meet these loved ones until we met in a world where there is no parting. I almost repined at the kind providence that had afflicted me and caused a separation between me and those I loved best. But 'tis better that I go from them a few months now than by staying *now* to go from them forever by and by. I lingered as long as possible among the familiar places of home and there with a sudden effort as I heard the carriage coming bade them all adieu. The last sad farewell was spoken the last lingering look was given. The last grasp of warm hands & adieus breathed by warmer hearts were all made, and I had received perhaps my last blessing from a kind father & affectionate mother.

Oh! how bitterly I wept as thoughts of happy hours spent in that home came rolling over me. Father, Mother, Wife, Child, Brothers, Sister, to all a kind though a sad farewell— May God watch over you & if we meet no more on earth may we all meet in a heaven of eternal rest.

Oct 13th Reached *Rome* today after the usual fatigue of a long passage over a northern railroad. We found the usual amount of mud & rain, & suffered the usual horrors of a lodging in a country tavern. Slept as usual in beds already occupied by bipeds, quadrupeds & insects. We were blest with good appetites and gratified them on such meagre bits of pork, hams & vegetables as usually fall to the share of such wayfarers as ourselves. And we all arrived at Rome as battered & bruised specimens of humanity as ever travelled over corduroy railroads.

Oct 14th to 16th Enjoying the small pleasure of a trip from Rome to New York & all its inconveniences. Went by way of Troy to avoid fatigue. Was troubled most of the way with a severe pain in my side and am sure I shall feel very thankful when we come in sight of the goodly city of Gotham. The very crankling noise of this steamer & the horrid buz of her coal blower make me sadly nervous. But time cures all ills & I expect he will cure my "ennui."

Oct 17th We arrived at the dock at 4 a.m. and I was suddenly aroused from my sleep by the jamming of the boat against the wharf, dressed and came on deck and was greeted by the usual number of carmen & cabmen, niggers & loafers, porters & thieves, all mingled in a heterogeneous mass. You could hear every variety of voice from the shrill sharp voice of the Frenchman to the coarse bass of the son of Kill-

4

kerney: "cab sir," "nice hack sir," "gemman goes with me," "city porter sir" were echoed and re-echoed on every side. Wedging my way through I went to the Clinton Hotel. New York is one of the strangest of cities. Every nation, tongue & kindred under the whole heaven seem to have found a home here. Black, White & Yellow all mingle together in a heterogeneous compound. Broadway is a world in itself and I delight to gaze on its busy bustling throng of restless mortals. After a great deal of fatigue & trouble have found a ship, the Lancashire & we shall sail on Thursday the 19th.

October 19. As it was my last day on shore I rose early, if possible to enjoy as long as I could the land. At breakfast ate but little, for my coffee would go down the wrong way and my food had a strange propensity to choke me. Went on board the Lancashire at 9 o'clock and took the tow boat at 10 to tow us out to sea. All seemed strangely new to me. The merry "yo heave ho" of the sailors as they hauled anchor, the hoisting of sails, the variety of orders and counter orders, all this novelty tended to wear away my melancholy. At 12 our pilot left us and altho' an utter stranger to me yet I hated to part with him, for he seemed the only link that bound us to land. We had a fine fresh breeze and soon lost sight of land. I stood on the quarter deck until the last speck had faded away in the distance and then I went below to give vent to my sorrowful feelings in tears.

"The Lancashire" is one of the first class American merchantmen of 800 tons burden and built at a cost of $50,000 or $60,000. She is 140 feet in length and 30 feet wide, having six large state rooms in our cabin and a beautiful steerage amidships. Capt. Lyon her commander is a thorough bred sailor and a gentleman, who by his kind attentions and gentlemanly behaviour endears himself to all who know him. He appears to love his home very much. As he came on board I casually remarked "Capt. Lyon, I suppose you are never sad at leaving land." The tears started from his eyes as he replied, "Ah! yes I am, for all I love are behind." I regretted much that I should have thus pained the heart of such a man, by awakening home thoughts & feelings. Our first mate Mr. Eckford is an English sailor, a real sea fowl; having always followed the sea he is unacquainted with the requirements of fashion & gentility, yet he is possessed of a nobler and better politeness that springs from a warm & generous heart. Our second mate is a Swede, a coarse sailer and a man much inferior to either of the others. Our crew, like most, is made up of the odds & ends of all creation. Every nation appears to have a representative on the Lancashire. English, Irish, Scotch, Swedes, Germans, French, Spanish, Indian & Negro all here find a common level. Black & White, friends & enemies, here find a home. What a strange compound is a sailor. A man whose residence is the wide world, whose home is the ocean's billow. Possessed of no local habitation he has no local feelings, no home attachments. He finds a home in every port, is warmly met and kindly greeted by vampires who only desire to fleece his pocket, and when destitute he is again sent forth to seek for further means in order to gratify the rapacity of a selfish landlord. His life is one scene of change and, I might add, of unmitigated hardship. Despised by those who reap most benefits from his services, he lives through this life without a hope that extends beyond today. The sailor is one of those strange beings who never profit by experience. This day is as yesterday & the moneys earned this year are sent in pursuit of those squandered the year before. If he lives to old age he may obtain a place in an alms house or become a street beggar. But generally he (who so loved the sea in his life time) finds a watery grave. None mourn his loss, a prayer is read by the captain, each tar responds amen, & then he is forgotten. Christianity & the holy influences of religion can alone elevate the character of the sailor. Our fine ship proves an excellent sailor & we are dashing ahead in fine style & we have literally "A wet sheet & a flowing sea." Have just witnessed a sunset at sea. Beautiful, beautiful, beyond the power of language to express. Often have I watched the glories of other sunsets but never seen ought that could compare with this. Would I were a painter & could transfer it to the canvass.

October 20th Friday. This is to me as unlucky a day as ever a Friday was to man for here I am suffering all the horrors of seasickness. I would not wish an enemy's dog a sorer punishment than this deadly seasickness. This turning a man wrong side out is anything but pleasant, to say nothing of the disagreeable appearances of such an operation. I do not know as I had a desire or fear while under its influence. Our fair wind has changed to a head wind and we are making a slow progress. Everything at sea is "mighty unsartin," so the old negro said & so it proves, for instead of nine knots an hour on our direct course here we are running off to sea and perhaps not making ½ a mile an hour towards Savannah. Our steward is a cross eyed Spaniard or, as the sailors say, "a double eyed son of gun" fitted expressly to keep both starboard & larboard watches. He provides very well & as I bribed him I am like to do very well indeed. As my seasickness wears away I find a great deal of amusement in watching the porpoises dance about our good ship.

October 21. A little ground bird alighted today on our crosstrees. Poor thing, she has undoubtedly been blown to sea by the westerly winds. She seems wearied with her long flight. Dear bird, like the dove who went forth from the ark, you find no resting place. Would I could send thee to my distant home to tell them of my welfare. Hast thou come from them to tell me of their happiness and health? Fare thee well, dear bird, may a fair wind waft thee to thy pleasant home. It seems strangely strange to look about me & see nought but "the sea, the sea, the open sea." Last night I felt much better of my sickness, and spent an hour or two walking in the cool night air with the mate of our vessel. I rallied him on his sober & sedate looks and then he confided to me all his sorrows. He is lately married in New York to a young & he says beautiful girl and was obliged to bid her adieu even before the honeymoon was over. He wept as he told me the little story of his ladie love who was far away. I was surprised to see such warm & ardent affection in such a coarse & rough sailor. He doubtless feels all the anxieties & cares I feel as I think of my loved ones who are absent. Thus it is, we often find the purest gem concealed by the coarsest exterior—and here in this poor sailor was love as strong as man ever felt for woman. We have about 50 Irish in the steerage & they have today got up a dance to the music of an old cracked flute & the way their old bedtick breeches cut it down the middle & cross over is a caution to all green ones. They are real Paddys fresh from the bogs of Killkerney and can shake their india rubber heels so as to frighten anyone except a genuine Corkonian.

Oct 22nd Sunday Is it possible that this day so full of bustle on ship board is the holy quiet Sabbath—the day of sacred rest. The decks are washed down today as every day, the sails are furled, reefed & unfurled today as on every other day & nought can distinguish it from any other day except the clean & neat appearance of the sailors. Tis 10½ o'clock & no sabbath bell greets my ear, inviting me to the house of prayer. Would I could step into my little room & greet you all this morning, and walk with my dear wife to the house of God. But no, I cannot. I can only listen to the changing of the watches, the orders of the Capt., the singing of the sailors as they tack ship. But God is here amid all this confusion & can hear my prayer in behalf of loved friends on shore.

October 23, 1843 The appearance of the sea at night is very beautiful, and as the waves break around our ship they resemble a sea of fire. It is supposed to be caused by the presence of animalculae—which give to the water this phosphoric appearance. We had quite a severe squall today & the wind is changing in our favour, so our good ship is bounding away towards our port. Saw some whales today at daylight (we are nearly 200 miles out at sea). I was much amused at the gambols of these huge monsters of the sea. I have recovered from my seasickness and am beginning to enjoy myself. Have been trying to learn the names of the sails & ropes, and took a run up the shrouds, but directly my head began to swim & I came down quite satisfied with being only a passenger.

Oct 24, 1843 I find our fair wind has again deserted us & here we have again a wind ahead. Patience—patience— have thy perfect work. Had a long talk today with Robert, an intelligent English sailor, on the folly of squandering his wages so foolishly. He heard me through my harangue very impatiently and said, giving his breeches a hitch & at the same time squirting from his mouth a half a pint of tobacco juice, "The devil is in it that you landsmen are always rating us so on keeping our weather eye open. You'd have us stow away every shot in the locker & never have a bit of a shindy on shore. You want us to save our money for some landlubber to cheat us out of. No! No!, said he, touching his hat, ours is a short life & we'll make it a merry one. By & by poor Jack will tip up on the crosstrees & away he's gone & then it's not much good his money'll do him." Strange! Such is the reasoning of 9/10 of all sailors on monetary affairs. Saw some sharks off to the windward and on observing to Johnny, an Irish sailor that stood by, "They are horrible animals," "Arrah!" said he, "& well may you say that same, but the devil has mony a worse shark on shore." True, thought I, his answer is correct, for these brutes only prey on others but man preys on his fellow. The one is guided by instinct & the other professes to be guided by reason.

Oct 25th I have had for some days a strong desire to visit the forecastle & last evening I took the opportunity. As I was descending the ladder, a sailor espied me & sung out, "Gemmen come to see Jack tar, make room." I briefly told them I only desired to see how they lived, that if I was a landlubber I loved to hear sailors sing & spin yarns & hoped they would go on as if I were not present. After a little time I begged a song & one song followed another & one yarn another until the evening was far spent & I retired thanking them for their songs and stories. Long shall I remember my visit to the forecastle and the kind freehearted welcome given me by the sailors. Have had some fine music today from the sailors & Irish. I do love a good bold song, sung in a free & cheerful voice. Saw Charlestown pilot boats today. Wind ahead and here we are only 80 or 90 miles from our port, but unless the wind changes no hopes of ever reaching there. Saw more

salt water sharks today & was much edified by a long yarn
of a shark story from our Capt. Too tough and too long to
insert here in my journal. Rains very hard and our captain
looks crabbed & sour. How mournfully the wind howls
through the rigging and all portends a dismal blow.

Oct 26 Have been sailing 24 hours and here we are not 4
miles further south than we were yesterday. Have a good
opportunity of watching and I am fully convinced that a
sailor's life is a dog's life with none of his pleasures. The Capt.
is the King and they are the subjects & the government is an
absolute monarchy. I have been on board seven days and I
have not seen Capt. Lyon speak to any one of the men. He
gives his orders & the mates see them executed. These sailors
are many of them fine looking men but they have not a
single hope for the future. They are slaves on ship and brutes
on shore. Capt. L treats his men well but yet there is a great
gulf between him & the men. May I & mine ever be delivered
from the debasement of a sailor's life.

Oct 27. Took a pilot today soon after daylight and all felt
more cheerful & contented, for altho' it does not secure a
sooner entrance to port, yet all are prone to believe that when
the pilot is on board the voyage has ended. Our pilot is a
fine, hale, hearty man of 66 years of age & quite fleshy enough
to pass for an Alderman. He has been engaged here as a pilot
for more than 40 years. The old weather beaten fowl is a
natural curiosity. His name is Broughton. It is one of those
cold, dismal, rainy days that give one the blues & serve to
make even the best society cheerless & unsociable. By the
by, here I have been a whole week on ship board and no description of my fellow passengers, & I have been rattling away
as if I were the only being in the universe. No. 1. Mr. Smith

of Savannah, a thick set, pleasant featured man, who has a very happy faculty of perpetrating a joke & tells a good story with a great deal of humour. Mr. S. is a slave holder &, I think, a candid upright man. He is occasionally rather hard on abolitionists & exhibits a little pique at their Yankee habit of meddling with others' business. Mr. Cochran of New York is No. 2, a dull, sleepy looking fellow, a great punster, & much addicted to good living & brandy & water. Mr. Heineman & Lady of Savannah—Germans by birth—are our No. 3 & 4 and very agreeable & pleasant companions they are. Mr. H is a gentleman who has travelled much & evidently has improved by his long intercourse with the world. Mr. Reed, No. 5, is a farmer of New York, clever & agreeable, is about becoming a southern planter. Of the remainder of the party I had not better venture a description but being selfishly interested we will venture to call them passable.

Oct 28, 1843 At daylight we came in sight of Tybee lighthouse and I need not say we were all rejoiced at the sight. It is a beautiful day & we already feel the balm sunny air of the south. How homelike the land seems after only a nine days of absence on the stormy sea. The lighthouse is, I believe, situated on an island. Already does the scenery look foreign. The harbour is a very good one and affords a safe anchorage to ships. We are only 18 miles from Savannah. The scenery on either side of the Savannah River is beautiful. The large rice plantations here & there ornamented with small groves of trees afford to the stranger a beautiful view. Your eye can see miles & miles over the lowlands, fertile & rich lands occupied in the raising of rice, & here & there a small bluff covered with trees rises looking like oasis in a desert. The dark skins that are seen in such masses on the plantations forcibly remind me that this is not home, but a land of slaves. The first slave I saw gave me the strangest sensations I ever experienced and like a curious Yankee who sees a great curiosity for the first time I longed to touch & examine to see if indeed these were men made of flesh and blood like myself. I gazed on them o'er and over again & wondered if these could be beings who never in their lives drew a breath of freedom. The slaves seem well fed and are generally well clothed. They seem an idle lazy race of beings & appear happy & contented. Already have we passed some 20 or 30 plantation boats rowed by these negroes singing merrily "Lucy Long" or "Jim Crow." Thus far all is new, all is strange, & I seem like a being suddenly transfer'd to a stranger land. The river is very tortuous & winds its way quietly to the ocean. Left our ship some 2 miles from the city & took our small boats up to the city, & I really felt feelings quite like sorrow at leaving the old ship, for it had been a home for me amid storms & tempests. As you approach the city of Savannah you lose sight of its spires & seem to approach a quiet village intrenched about with trees. The streets are very sandy & was very glad to come to an anchor in the Pulaski house—where I shall while away the day in writing home letters to friends.

Oct 29th & 30th *Savannah* is a very pleasant city situated on a beautiful bluff some 60 or 70 feet above the river & commands a fine view of the river harbour & surrounding country. The houses are old & of a very bad style yet I should think well adapted to a southern climate, being mostly built of brick. The place is very regularly laid out in squares and the streets are wide & airy, bordered by beautiful shade trees. This plan gives to all beautiful locations & equalizes the advantages of the city. There are I believe 20 squares in the city. This plan of "rus in urbe" is delightfully adapted to a southern climate and shows the wisdom of the early colonists who first settled here. The city has but few curiosities. A fine plain monument has been erected to the memory of Pulaski & Greene. There is a fine old cemetery here that is a curiosity to strangers. Every kind of labour is performed by blacks and it invariably takes a half a dozen blacks to do what one white would. They seem happy & cheerful & slavery does not appear a yoke to many of them. I am much amused at the variety of colour exhibited here & which shows too clearly the loose morals of at least some part of the population. I visited the market on Saturday evening & found much amusement in the trafficking of the negroes with each other (it was after the whites had finished their marketing). Some were singing, some laughing, some bantering, all full of life & activity. Cries of all kinds greeted my ears in the peculiar dialect of these negroes. "Yaw nigar, you no guine to cheat dis ole darky," said one. "He neber do, nohow dem taters don't," said another. "Dis de ole child to buy fish ob," cried a fish monger. &c. &c. to the end of the chapter. Sunday I heard Bishop Elliott of Georgia & was much pleased with his calm & impressive manner. He was exceedingly eloquent. His subject the dangers of Unitarianism. The Pulaski House is one of the best kept hotels in the United States, where you are served with every luxury. They have a faculty of endearing themselves to all strangers by their horrible exorbitant charges. I have enjoyed my stay in Savannah very much & am delighted with its climate. Here I have seen orange & fig trees bearing fruit. It is said to be one of the best climates in the United States altho' they have occasionally the yellow fever. There are 2 cases here now.

October 31. We left the pleasant city of Savannah yesterday in the Steamer Genl Taylor for St. Augustine. Our little craft is only about the size of a Brooklyn ferry boat & seems illy fitted to contend with the wind & wave. We have taken the inland passage & find the scenery beautiful & the air as mild & balmy as that of Italy. The tropical trees grow here in abundance & their foliage is rich & beautiful. We have a large party of officers on board & some of them are very gentlemanly, well bred men. Others appear to have taken that place only through the magic of gilding & lace. Genl Worth's family were among our fellow passengers & I was much pleased with their appearance. I am heartily sick of travelling & shall be delighted to set my feet again on shore. I am very anxious to hear from my home which I expect to do at St Augustine. We arrived at St Augustine at about 2 o'clock today & had I have [*sic*] suddenly awoke from sleep I should have imagined I was a denizen of some old city in the old world. So antiquated does this place seem one might well suppose it had been built by Noah. I asked the nigger steering the boat "if this was an old place" only wishing to hear his answer. "Ole, I guess he is, very decrepit place massa," he replied & I enjoyed the blunder very much. There was a large crowd of officers & negroes, Spaniards, soldiers, & Minorcans at the wharf.[1] Friends greeted friends & as the notes of welcome given to others fell on my ear I felt with all its force that I was indeed a stranger in a strange land. Would some kind fairy hand could transfer my wife here so I too could have some one to welcome me to the shore. I was soon aroused by the voice of a negro "Florida House, Sar." "Yes," I replied &

---

[1] These were descendants of indentured settlers planted at New Smyrna in 1767 by Dr. Andrew Turnbull in partnership with Sir William Duncan and Sir Richard Temple. An account of the undertaking is in Carita Doggett (Corse), *Dr. Andrew Turnbull and the New Smyrna Colony of Florida* (1919).

giving him my luggage I started. At first I imagined my guide was taking me through some back lane by a nearer way but soon I found that all streets were alike & that this was one of the main streets in St. Augustine. I am settled in a dismal room at the Florida House full of melancholy & sad thoughts.

Nov 1st *St Augustine* is one of the oldest places in the United States & was first settled by the Spaniards. It was laid out after the plan of old Castilian cities. The streets or lanes are very narrow indeed. When I first saw two carts meet in the street I watched with some anxiety to see what course would be followed. Two carriages can just pass & foot travellers must keep a careful watch or they may be run down by some careless driver. Sidewalks are entirely unknown & all alike wade through the sand & dust. The houses are situated immediately on the street & this gives a much more dark & dismal appearance to the street. Most of the houses have a piazza built out from the 2d story & if the houses were directly opposite you could easily step from one house to the other across the street. The place seems destitute of all ideas of modern civilized architecture and no stranger can imagine the ancient appearance of these old Spanish houses. The Minorcan residences are generally still worse, being built like barns with steep roofs & heavy shutters & they remind one of a lot of old rookeries. I find that if the demands of taste are not attended to the demands of appetite are, for we live well on fish & game &c &c. Bade adieu to my dismal room at the Florida House this afternoon & have found a pleasant boarding place at Mrs. Reid's, widow of the late Governor Reid. Mrs. R is a very pleasant & agreeable lady & I think I may consider myself fortunate in procuring so good a home. Would my dear wife & child were here to make it indeed a home. Mrs. Reid has the happiest negroes I have seen & they come up to you so pleasantly & say "what you have massa"; it really amuses me. I asked the negro boy who waits on us what his name was. "Dey calls me Sawney for short but my name is John." I had the curiosity today to measure one of the old streets & found it only three paces wide. Another was only five paces & that is, I think, the widest street in St. Augustine. One of the streets is so narrow you can stand in its centre & touch either side.

Nov 2, 1843 The *streets of St Augustine* are laid out without any reference to regularity or beauty & seem as you look on them from an eminence as so many snakes twisting in with each other. In the centre of the city fronting the bay & harbour is a large square & in its centre an old looking monument that compares well with the ancient appearance of the place. On the west side of the square is the present court house, formerly the Governor's house & Depository of the Public archives. It looks like an old weatherbeaten castle more than the abode of justice. On the north side is the Old Catholic church with one of the most quaint looking fronts I have ever seen. It resembles the architecture of old cathedrals built in the 17th century. The market place & other buildings on the square possess no novelty or interest. I visited today an old ruin near the square once the residence of the Spanish Governor. It is built of stone with arched windows & ceilings & reminds one of Stevens' researches in Central America. There is a court & well in the centre after the manner of dwellings in the east. On my way home met a very aged decrepit negro, one of the oldest persons I ever saw. "How old are you," said I. "Me no know, massa, Buckra man steal niggar year year ago." He seemed worn out with a life

17

of toil in the service of another but yet was cheerful & happy. His life has been a dark one & he will soon go to a place of eternal rest.

Nov 3, 1843 I have today visited the *old Spanish fortification* at this place and it is a great curiosity.[2] It is built in the form of a polygon with four bastions & four equal curtains. It is built on flat ground a little above high water mark in the north part of the town. It is built of a species of shell stone found in great abundance near here & is the only fort of the kind in the United States. The fort is surrounded by a deep ditch or trench & undoubtedly at one time had drawbridges at its main entrances. It has a large area in the centre & is mounted with four towers from which you have an extended view of the bar, bay & harbour. The walls & terraces are covered with an exceeding durable cement which is still in many places in a perfect state of preservation. As you enter the fort through a long arched room you see, on either side, other rooms of a similar character 25 or 30 feet high with a narrow aperture at the top for the admission of light and air, & out of these are dungeons of the darkest and most dismal character. The western part of the fort is now occupied by criminals as a state's prison. In the eastern part of the fort is one of the most horrible of dungeons, which was only discovered a few years since & in it was found the skeleton of some poor wretch who perished a victim to Spanish cruelty. His history will never be known.

You reach the top of the fort by means of an arched way from the inner court covered with cement which still is as

---

[2] The Fort of San Marco, built of coquina, a soft stone formed of cemented shell and pebbles which was quarried on Anastasia Island, was in course of construction from 1672 to 1756. Jeanette Thurber Conner, "The Nine Old Wooden Forts of St. Augustine," *Florida Historical Society Quarterly,* 4:103–11, 171–80; for the stone fort itself, pp. 175–80.

perfect as when first built. This fort with but little repairs would seem impregnable. It was from this fort that Wild Cat and his warriors escaped during the late war & it is astonishing to think how he could escape through one of these narrow windows some 30 feet from the floor & some 40 feet from the ditch.[3] Would the noble Osceola could have escaped with you & not have fallen a victim to white men's perfidy. This old fort is a relic of antiquity which is seldom seen in our cities & at once carries the beholder back to the days of Ferdinand. It seems as if at every turn you would meet some steel clad soldier knight or hear the challenge of some dark mustashd soldier. On the outer wall over the gateway is the court of arms & under it an inscription which is now nearly effaced. On the opposite side of the moat is an altar, with a cross & lamb attached, affixed to a similar court of arms; there are three steps to this altar built of this soft stone & are very much worn in the centre, a place about as large as a man's knee, supposed to have been worn by devotees kneeling before their altar. This fortification was many years in building & was built mostly by the labour of convicts & slaves from Mexico & Cuba & cost the King of Spain an immense sum of money. A good story is related that when the King heard of its completion he took his spy glass & went to a high eminence expecting to see the fort towering up to heaven, thinking that the subject of so much labour & expense ought to be seen from across the Atlantic.

Nov 4. Mrs. Reid has given me an interesting a/c of *Osceola* the Indian Chief who was for a long time confined

[3] Cooacoochee, "son of Philip, the principal chief on the St. John's River," made his escape from the fort. Joshua R. Giddings in *The Exiles of Florida* (Columbus, 1858), pp. 168–69, gives an account in Wild Cat's own words as reported by Captain Sprague.

here.[4] He was a noble hearted being, frank, generous & high-minded, yet revengeful to his enemies. His capture was only effected by the vilest fraud which ought forever to brand with infamy those who were the chief actors in the scene. He was invited to come in & have a friendly talk, protestations of friendship were made by the whites, and Osceola who was undoubtedly anxious to see this war honorably ended came in with 30 of his warriors to have a friendly council, and in order to show what confidence he had in the whites, they left all their weapons behind & came unarmed. And while General Hernandez was making protestations of the warmest friendship Gen[l] Jessup surrounded them & brought them all in prisoners. Osceola & his band were brought to St. Augustine & altho' every citizen was anxious to see this bloody war closed, yet so ashamed were all of the perfidious treachery of the whites that no one gave way to rejoicing or exultation but perfect silence prevailed except the measured tread of the soldiers & the heavy tramp of the horses. Osceola looked the noblest there & the lightning of his eye said "you would not have me here except through deceit." When placed in confinement he drooped & died. He never smiled but his face was always as calm & stern as a marble statue, at times he seemed wan & dejected. Doubtless his heart was far away with the loved ones of his native home. He died of a broken heart, another victim to the treachery of a white man's friendship. No doubt the Indians were malignant & cruel, yet they fought

[4] "In the dishonorable record of our dealings with the Indians there is perhaps no blacker chapter than that relating to the Seminole people." Grant Foreman, *Indian Removal* (University of Oklahoma Press, Norman, 1932), p. 315. An outcome of the Indian removal policy of the Jackson administration, the Second Seminole War (1835–42) was characterized by the usual treaty with a part of the chiefs for the surrender of lands not at the time demanded or needed for settlement by whites, by unusual suffering and mortality among the tribesmen who actually did go to the western lands, and by unprecedented treachery and deceit practiced by the whites upon those who refused to migrate. The story is told by Joshua R.

as did our sires for home & country, they loved as did our
fathers the scenes of childhood & the graves of their fathers.
When will the cupidity & cruelty of white men cease. Never,
no never till the last lone Indian has gone to the spirit land.

Nov 5 1843. Today is the Sabbath. Went to our church
and heard a beautiful discourse from the rector of the parish.
The Sabbath is better observed here than in most southern
cities and an air of quiet & repose is spread over everything.
It is communion day & we had an interesting season. In the
after part of the day 3 Black children were baptised. It was
to me a deeply interesting sight. I never witnessed a deeper
humility than was exhibited by these poor slaves. They did
not dare to kneel on the cushioned step before the altar but
knelt on the floor. These Blacks have a deep reverence for religion & all its sacraments. They think it their duty to have their
grave clothes in readiness before they die & the older negroes
make it one great object of life to save enough money to buy
a good suit of habiliments for the grave & when ready they say
in answer to any question about their worldly prosperity
"tank God me get along well. Me got all ob de clothes ready
& wheneber de Lor call me all ready to lay dis ole body in de
ground." Would it not be well if we all thought more often
of the grave whither we go. A large portion of this population

Giddings in *The Exiles of Florida*, where there is perhaps quite as much concern
for the Negroes involved as for the Indians; it is also told in a more dispassionate
manner by Grant Foreman in *Indian Removal*, especially chapters 25–31.

Quoting from correspondence copied in the *Army and Navy Chronicle* (2:197),
Foreman (p. 328) reproduces a word picture of Osceola, or Powell, as he was also
called, for his father was an Englishman: ". . . an upstart in the nation; but one
who has obtained his present high elevation by his energy and his talents . . ."
It is possible that Whipple may have seen this description which appeared first in
the *Newbern* (North Carolina) *Spectator* in February, 1836. However that may be,
there is a remarkable similarity between his characterization and that in the North
Carolina newspaper. Interesting sidelights on the early part of the Seminole War
are in *Sketch of the Seminole War, and Sketches during a Campaign*, by a Lieutenant of the Left Wing (Charleston, South Carolina, 1856).

are slaves & they are generally of a kind & indolent temper. The Catholics form another large portion of the population & nothing can equal their strict attendance upon the ordinances of their religion. They put to shame too often the less rigid followers of a pure religion. Would their quiet zeal & devoted lives were spent in spreading the glorious gospel of Christ unshackled by monkish superstitions.[5]

Nov 6, 1843 I have called on Genl Worth & presented him my letter of introduction.[6] I was much pleased with his frank gentlemanly demeanor & his kind hearty welcome. Genl W is a man justly esteemed for his skill in closing amicably the hazardous Indian Wars of Florida. He did it with much honor to himself & to his country. The business men of St. Augustine appear to me to be generally divested of that straightforward upright character that should characterize a merchant. Jockeying, cheating & bantering appear too common & all prices for goods are exorbitantly high. I have formed some pleasant acquaintances & do not feel as lonely as I did, altho' no new friends can make good the place of the dear ones left at home. Today is the election day & I have had some sport in watching the speckled, coloured & streaked appearance of the voters who form the population of the antique city of St. Augustine. Fighting, swearing & drinking

[5] According to his granddaughter, Mrs. Jane Whipple Burt, the Bishop's attitude toward Catholicism became much modified in his later life. Indeed, he became, in her words, a close friend of Archbishop Ireland.

[6] It was Colonel William Jenkins Worth (1794–1849) who, April 19, 1842, finally defeated the Seminole at Palaklaklaha. He was still in Florida commanding the Eighth Infantry. Worth entered the regular army as a first lieutenant in 1813, served through the War of 1812, to emerge a major as a result of his conduct at Lundy's Lane, where he was wounded. In 1838 he was made colonel and placed in command of the Eighth Infantry. Subsequently he served in the Mexican War under both Taylor and Scott and was brevetted Brigadier General for his distinguished conduct at Monterey. After the Mexican War he was in command of the Department of Texas until his death.

with the other usual accompaniments of a southern election were served up in abundance & almost made one blush at such a specimen of republicanism. The party who beat had a glorification in the evening and marched through the streets singing & laughing, their music being occasionally diversified by the sound of a cracked tamborine. There are in St. Augustine some old ruins of the Moorish order of architecture that are rich treats to those who possess a taste for antiquities. Stevens might easily transfer their sketches to his antiquities and no one detect the deceit. There are a few fine groves of orange trees in the vicinity of St. Augustine & these tropical plants in full bloom look singular enough to one accustomed to our northern winters. Most plants are evergreens here & we escape the mournful sensations caused by the falling leaves. Have today received a letter from my dear home & again feel happy in knowing that those I love so well were happy.

Nov 8. There was formerly a convent in this place, the convent of San Francisco, now fitted up for the United States Barracks. These Barracks are now occupied by the 8th Regiment under command of Gen.l Worth. I sometimes while away an hour or two in listening to the fine stirring martial music played by the band at early morn & evening. My only amusement has thus far been to walk & this is already becoming a stale business. The weather is very warm, thermometer from 75 to 80—and no doubt at home they are all freezing from cold.

Nov 13 Today desired to get a boat and asked a negro present if he knew where the Minorcan lived who owned them & asked him if they would lend them. "Lend un, massa, by gosh dem Minorcan neber lend he boat. He looka very

much like white man but you find he anoder animal." So it is.
These Minorcans live by fishing, except the better class, and
you might as well ask for his household Gods as to ask the
loan of his boat. Finally procured a boat & had a beautiful
sail down the brack, walked several miles & found a beautiful
star fish, which I have preserved. We have beautiful weather,
a fine balmy air & excellent living. Tomato's, radishes, lettuce
& greens & fruit in abundance and plenty of fish, oysters &c.
Have nothing to do & time begins to hang heavily & puts me
in mind often that this is not home. Would it were & I could
see my beloved ones again. I was much amused today in
watching the pelicans by hundreds marching like an army in
battle array upon the beach. Snipes, ducks & other game are
here in abundance. This week is court week and I shall attend
& see how justice is administered in Florida.

Nov 15. Have attended *court* until I am tired. Law appears to be rather a hard commodity here. The juries deal
summarily with all cases & despatch them quickly, a little on
the order of old English courts where the verdict was sometimes settled by flipping a copper. The classifications of crimes
is singular. Manslaughter, bigamy & falsely packing cotton
are under one head. Murder here costs about 2 years imprisonment or $1000 fine. Altho they have excellent judges, yet
such juries as they have here are beyond any man's control.
The weather looks foggy and like a storm. The juries look as
if made up of scant materials where all the stock on hand
was worked in. A more motley group I have never seen than
today in the jury room. Such an assortment of character as I
will wager could only be found in Florida. During the recess
of court one of the grand jury men came below & found his
hopeful son of some 8 or 9 years of age fighting with another

boy. The father looked coolly on until it was ended and then said "Now you little devil, if you catch him down again bite him, chaw his lip or you never'll be a man." Really a singular character to guard over the peace & well being of the country but only one of the numerous specimens of this fighting spirit only to be found in the south. But a few years since & this fighting spirit was so prevalent that it was necessary for a man to keep a double guard on his tongue, else he might be called out by some of these worthies.

Nov 16. Had a delightful sail today down the harbor & had a beautiful walk on the ocean beach. How many thrilling thoughts come rushing through one's mind as we stand on the ocean shore and gaze on its vast & heaving bosom. No place so fit for man to feel his littleness & blush to think that he, a worm, an atom, a speck upon the earth, should ever dare to indulge in pride or arrogance. The air & climate of St. Augustine is one of the finest in the world & were it home I would love to live & die in this sunny land, this land of flowers as it is named. The soil of St. Augustine & its vicinity is sandy yet is very productive indeed. It has in its ingredient a large portion of carl lime & other compositions that make it entirely unlike the sand of Georgia & New York. I was astonished to see the enormous growth of squashes, pumpkins, potatoes &c upon this apparently dry & barren soil. Have had a long conversation today with a large party from Alabama who are hunting land. They have travelled over the northern part of Florida and say the land is extremely good, generally of a sandy character except in the oak & hickory ridges & there of a clayey character. In many tracts you find a rich loam equal in fertility to the Mohawk & Genesee valleys. Even a very large portion of the everglades can be drained &

then there is not a richer soil in the world. Took a delightful ride out into the country four or five miles & was somewhat astonished to find so near this old city so wild & new a country. After leaving St. Augustine you soon enter the pine barrens— land covered with pine trees so open you can ride miles & miles in any direction. The day was beautiful and I found my ride exhilarating & pleasant. Rode on the route past the plantation of Col. Hanson & here I saw the first sugar cane I have seen since I have been south. It resembles our corn & looks well when in full growth as at present. The crop is now about ready for harvest. It is planted in January & is a long time in coming to maturity. Life on a plantation is full of interest to a stranger. All is new, the luxuriance of the crops, the droves of slaves & quantities of barelegged young negroes seem singular enough. The slaves on this plantation are well dressed & seem happy. The scenery here is beautiful & the changing of the scene from time to time adds to it an interest not to be found in the north. I have noticed today a large number of the Spanish bayonet trees & have seen a hedge planted of them & they seem well adapted for such a purpose. At every step you take you see something new to please & interest you & remind you you are in the sunny south. The air of this climate is indeed delightful in the extreme. Life here is so different from that at the north. Here I am in my thin summer dress writing by an open window while at the north my friends are doubtless shivering by a blazing fire.

November 18th 1843 The *inhabitants of Florida* are rapidly improving in character from the continual influx of new settlers from other states and that coarse rough backwoods crackerism is giving place to refinement & civilization. But a few years since and Florida was common ground for southern blacklegs and desperados, but they are fast disappearing. The law is now better regarded and good citizens are exerting themselves to give character & standing to the territory. Occasionally now, the people are compelled to witness the public fight & see those who ought to be gentlemen descend to the common bully. Witnessed a laughable trial today of one judge (Judge Smith) for having whipped another judge (Judge Gould) and was somewhat surprised to hear such scurrility and vulgarity allowed in a court of justice as was used by one of the parties. Judge Bronson charges a jury strongly in view of the right & does not allow himself to be browbeaten by anyone. I believe there are six indictments against individuals for fights at this session of court, showing the state of society in a sparse population. Among the population of Florida are large numbers of crackers from Georgia who have lately taken up lands here. Some of these fellows have a good deal of humor and have a happy faculty of making doggerel poetry. A gentleman whose name was N. Burrit was the other day teasing one of these fellows for rhymes. After a while the cracker commented

"God made a man & called him Nelson Burrit"
After he saw his face he was sorry for it"

thus turning a good joke on the lawyer his tormentor. Jails & state's prisons are novelties here. There is a comical jail in the Alachua district made of hewn logs with an opening at the top into which they drop the prisoner & thus render his escape impossible from his wolf trap. And it is said that formerly the judge in this new country was compelled to fasten culprits in rail fences for contempt of court as there was no other means of punishment. Today saw a splendid specimen of Florida jury. A man was arraigned for stealing wood (3 cords), clearly proved guilty and fined the enormous sum of

$10. This is the cheapest stealing I have ever seen, as the wood was worth $9, and the prisoner only loses $1.00 by his acquisitive propensities.

Nov 21. Left St. Augustine today in *Picolata* stage. The route is a dismal one as can be well imagined as the road lays through the woods and the land is poor pine barrens. A Job's patience would be tried through such a nondescript country as this. Our passengers were three residents of St. Augustine and an Indian guide who served through the Florida war in this Indian hunt. He rendered the ride very melancholy by pointing out every few rods the scenes of Indian massacre. This road as well as most others here is traced with blood. After five hours of as tedious riding as I ever experienced I reached Picolata. Here and there you pass through hammocks from which the Indians were wont to make their attacks & these bloody tales of our guide were not very pleasant especially to as nervous a being as myself. At Picolata (a city in the parlance of speculators) we found 3 or 4 houses and as desolate a looking place as can be seen. It resembles the Eden of Dickens' Martin Chuzzlewit. From Picolata we went to Black Creek in the St. Mathews and here found another of these Florida cities only famed for their desolate looking houses. The owl & bittern of Babylon might well weep over such loneliness. The scenery on Black Creek is monotonous in the extreme & the tall oaks and cypresses on its banks covered with hanging moss seem to weep over the desolation. The river St. Johns is one of the finest rivers in the U. S. The scenery is in some places romantic & beautiful. I saw some fine alligators basking in the sun 16 to 20 feet in length. They are hideous looking creatures, monsters of deformity. We stopped at Jacksonville a few hours and pro-

ceeded to St. Marys—Georgia. A few miles from St. Marys
we passed Cumberland Beach, so renowned as the theatre of
many bloody duels. It was here that Palosti and Babcock
fought.[7] Cruel horrid custom thus to butcher & destroy men
for the false code of honor. Honor! It is a vague idea the
duellist has of honor. He does not know whether its location
be in his head or heels.

Nov 24th St. Marys is a small place, pleasantly situated
upon the St. Mary's River and has a population of about 800.
It had a population of 900 at the last census but it has rapidly
decreased since that time owing to planters removing from
their exhausted plantations in Georgia to the new lands in
Florida. Its citizens appear to be very intelligent and hospitable. I have formed the acquaintance of Mr. Sadler &
Preston, two very pleasant and agreeable gentlemen. The
staples of the low country in Georgia are mainly cotton &
rice, altho' some of the planters have cultivated sugar extensively, but this crop is too exhausting in its nature for the
light lands of this section. The slaves here are well treated,
indeed were it not for the odium of the name, all men would
approve of its form here. The slave system here is regulated
much better than in most portions of the south. The slave has
his tasks assigned to him & after they are finished which is
generally soon after noon his time is his own to fish, hunt
or cultivate land for himself & the avails of which he can
spend in buying finery & necessaries for his family. He is
allowed a peck of corn per week and can raise fowls, keep a

[7] T. Frederick Davis in his *History of Jacksonville, Florida, and Its Vicinity,
1813–1924* (Florida Historical Society, 1925), p. 83, tells the same story except
that Babcock's opponent was a Dr. Pelot and not Palosti. The duel grew out of a
drunken quarrel and Pelot was killed. Davis states that the encounter took place on
Amelia Island and bases his story on what he says was written at the time by a
Jacksonville citizen.

pig &c for himself. Altho in the uplands they are allowed more food directly from the hand of his master, yet still this is more than counterbalanced by his time being entirely given up to the service of his master. The slaves are here allowed to attend church and are generally very religious. St. Marys appears to be a very moral place. The people are generally Presbyterians. I heard today of another instance of the barbarious manner which the Floridians have in settling difficulties. Two men had a slight difficulty about some hogs. They became enraged & meeting each other both fired at the same time. The one was killed & the other dangerously wounded. Such scenes may be worthy of Texas, but an American must blush at such scenes in this land of light & freedom.

Nov 25th The people of the southern states are generally much more hospitable than northerners, and this difference must be attributed mainly to the fact that they are not such a money loving people. You do not see that low mean cupidity, that base selfishness so striking a characteristic of one portion of our restless Yankee brethren. But the energies of the south are crippled by the incubus of slavery. Indeed, as John Randolph says, were it not that their staples are not liable to competition with free labor, they could not sustain themselves, for if it did planters would be obliged to run away from their slaves if the slave did not run away from the master. I regret deeply that blind fanaticism should so warp the judgment of any portion of our citizens that they will detract and abuse men naturally so noble hearted as the intelligent and educated planters at the south. They feel the evils of slavery, but to free the slave would be ruin to the master and destruction to the slave. I am more & more convinced that most of the exaggerated stories of abolitionists exist only in imagination.

And from personal observation I know that the efforts of abolitionists at the north have only served to injure the slave and to destroy that kind & fraternal feeling which should exist between the northern and southern states. The south are not blind to the evils of slavery, they can see its bad effects as well as the most sharp sighted abolitionists yet they cannot nor will they consent to have caustic remedies applied by unskillful hands which would only serve to increase rather than diminish the evil. No! if slavery ever is abolished it must be gradual and done at the desire of & in the manner which the slaveholder desires. The slaveholders are generally opposed to the internal slave trade, and the families of slaves are never separated unless owing to the embarrassed situation of the master.

This evening I took tea with Esq. H. R. Sadler and met there his accomplished daughter & Miss Clynch, Mr. Laud, Mr. Madison & Mr. & Mrs. Preston beside his wife and mother. The evening passed off pleasantly in agreeable conversation & in listening to the sweet music discoursed to us by Miss S. Mr. Sadler is a thorough bred gentleman, simple & unostentatious in his habits & kind & manly in his intercourse with others. He pleases all by his frankness & his intelligence. Mr. S. gave me an insight into his management as a planter. He said it was true the government of the planter is despotic, as despotic as can be. The will of the master is law, yet this is not only necessary but kindness to the slave on account of his indolent degraded condition. Each family is allowed a piece of ground to cultivate for himself (he has 40 or 50 acres thus appropriated) and each slave has his task, which is generally finished from 12 to 2 o'clock. After that his time is his own to plant & sow for himself and his slaves have this year all of six hundred bushels of corn for sale the avails of which

is entirely their own. They have the privilege of dancing, singing &c &c. I was much pleased with a very laughable account
Mr. Sadler gave me of a visit of his to New York some years
since and of the negro who waited on him. But as I intend
visiting his plantation I will not describe it farther until I see
for myself. Mr. S. says it is greatly for the interest of the master to treat the slave kindly and although there are some cases
of brutality at the south, yet we despise such men, said he, as
much as do you. He invited me to visit him often and to call
at his house whenever I could find time.

Nov 26, 1843 I accompanied Mr. Preston and several
other gentlemen today on a sailing excursion down to Fer-
nandina, a small settlement on the frontiers of Florida. We
passed Cumberland Beach & I had pointed out to me the place
where Babcock & Palosti fought, also on Amelia Island the
spot where Floyd & Hopkins fought. This last was one of the
bloodiest duels ever fought in this section of country.[8] The
arrangement was that each should be armed with a double
barrelled gun loaded with buck shot, with a pair of pistols &
a bowie knife. At the word they were to advance towards each
other and fire at such time as they pleased. If the guns failed
to kill they were to use the pistols & then finish with bowie
knives & fight until one or the other was killed. They fought
until both were very badly mutilated and then the seconds

[8]General John Floyd (1769–1839) was a well-known Georgian. He commanded
the militia called out by the governor to oppose the Seminole and Creek Indians in
1813. L. L. Knight, *A Standard History of Georgia and the Georgians*, 1:464, 514.
In 1814 he led an expedition against the Upper Creek; he was made major general
and commanded the forces at Savannah. Subsequently he served a number of
terms in the state legislature and was a member of Congress for the term 1827–29.
A. D. Chandler and C. A. Evans, eds., *Georgia, Comprising Sketches of Counties,
Towns, Events, Institutions, and Persons, Arranged in Cyclopedic Form* (Atlanta,
1906), 2:49–50. Hopkins seems to be preserved to history only as the opponent of
General Floyd.

separated them. This Genl Floyd resides about 20 miles from here & has quite an armory. He appears to desire to keep about him the days of chivalry of old. The Floridians fight on Cumberland Island & the Georgians fight on Amelia Island. The one is in Georgia the other is in Florida only separated by a few miles & thus they are enabled to evade all law. After we had rambled about a few hours we returned but as our wind had left us, two negroes, slaves of Mr. P rowed us back and gave us a specimen of negro lyrics. All of these blacks sing and generally they choose a lively tune & invent words as they need them. I caught a few snatches of their songs & insert them, as they are really amusing.

Dis ole niggar lub a gal, ha Misse Dinah ha
She roll her eye when dis niggar go by, ha Misse Dinah ha
She got an arm, dis made ob whalebun, ha Misse Dinah ha
She got a lips dis all ob honey, ho Misse Dinah ho
Her teeth is made ob ibory, ho Misse Dinah ho
She is as brack as my ole hat, ho Misse Dinah ho
I lub dis gal & she lub me, ho Misse Dinah ho

and other lines of a similar nature were made up praising his darky beauty ad infinitum. Another song was

Blow, boys, blow
Blow dis niggar of to New Yak, Blow Boys Blow
Dere he walk de streets, Blow Boys blow
Dere he kiss de gals, Blow Boys Blow
Dere he read de papers, Blow Boys Blow
Dere he cut his capers, Blow Boys Blow.

Another equally nonsensical was

De speckle taters cotch dis niggar, oh! deary oh!
Dey send im to Alabamo, oh! deary oh!
Dere dey flog dis niggar, oh! deary oh!

33

Dere dey roas dis niggar, oh! deary oh!
He neber cotch any possum, oh! deary oh! &c &c &c.

They have a horrible dread of being sold into the south-western states & many of their songs are about the horrors of those places. Their ear for music is good and they will sing in words which no one else could twist into music by accenting some syllables very much & others little. Many negroes give their master so much per month for their time & make what they can. They generally pay the master about $10 per month for their time. But altho' slavery may be less dreadful to the slave than many would fain make us believe, yet it is a curse to the whites. It prostrates the energy of the country & prevents the south from becoming that business country which it would have been had our fathers never imported slaves. And despite the assertions of others, I am fully confirmed in the belief that this is no place for the poor man. The tendency of the planting interest is to make the rich man richer & the poor man poorer.

Nov 28. Mr. Du Buske (a planter near Reids Bluff, Florida) invited me to go over the river with him & spend the night and the next day to accompany him to Nassau Court which was to be held on Thursday, Judge Bronson presiding, and as my friend Mr. Preston, a young lawyer of St. Marys, intended to be there I concluded to go. Mr. Griswold, formerly of Utica, accompanied us. We left St. Marys about 3 o'clock P. M. and walked nearly a mile & a half through bog & mire to a point on the river where he usually left his boat and there shipped ourselves for a cruise to Florida. Our boat was one of the cypress canoes so common here & for a long time I rode under the delightful apprehension of upsetting & becoming food either for sharks or alligators, a delectable

34

choice truly. Mr. Du Buske is a very agreeable man, somewhat witty & tells a story remarkably well. After a ride of
three or four miles we landed and again took to our trotters
through open pine land & here & there a little hammock for
a mile & a half & came in sight of his plantation. He has about
30 negroes & raises cotton. We found his house like most of
southern plantation houses in the woods, merely a good
frame boarded up and floors laid with lath partitions without
plastering but his table amply repaid the loss of a good northern house & I for one did it justice. We took a walk through
his plantation, visited his cotton house &c &c. The cotton crop
when ready for picking is a beautiful sight. You can see the
blossom, the bud & the staple ready for picking. In a good
season the plant will not grow more than 3 or 3½ feet high
altho' some of this was 7 feet and upwards. The cotton is
first picked from the boll in the field, then sorted at the cotton
house, then ginned and lastly packed for market. The blossom is a beautiful yellow or straw colour resembling very
much our holly hocks at the north and has about as much
fragrance. Mr. Dubuske will have a poor crop, only about
100lb to the acre. It is a very uncertain crop as almost every
element seems combined to destroy it and there is a small
red insect which ruins a great deal every year.

We spent the evening very pleasantly in listening to the
stories of Mr. Du Buske about negro habits and character. He
said that a few years since it was very common for negroes to
think that they had a call to preach and that many times it
was highly amusing to hear them. They loved to dwell on
high wrought descriptions of another state of existence of the
devil &c &c. He said that one Sunday a negro preacher was
holding forth to his slaves & he had a curiosity to listen. He
heard him describing the devil as follows "Belubed broder-

35

nen, since I'se had de occashun to spake ob de debul, let me gib you discripshun of him. De debul is grate brack man ges like my broder Simon, only more so. His eye be like a pewter bullet in a brack stump, his teete be like de new teete to de cross cut saw, his nose, de lighten stream from de nose and His posterior dewelopment smoke like a tar kiln." He said many times these black preachers are great rascals and the other blacks who are truly religious will not hear him. Mr. Du B's negroes are nearly all Baptists and very religious. As we retired to our rooms we could hear from the negro cabins their evening songs of praise to God.

Nov 30 We arose today very early to take a campaign to the Nassau Court house about twelve miles through the woods. Mr. Du B & G's took horses and in lieu of a horse I mounted a mule. Never did I laugh so merrily in my life. The quiet demure looking parson face of the animal, his long ears and solemn looks made me laugh heartily. You have doubtless seen in comic almanacs pictures of tall anatomies mounted on these long eared animals belabouring him to move him into a trot and he the meantime occasionally kicking by way of amusement. Mr. Preston joined us after riding a little way and we jogged along through the barren woods occasionally passing through hammocks and small pieces of swamp land & I warrant we were as jolly a cavalcade as e'er rode through Florida woods. I was two or three times taken all aback, as the sailors say, by seeing a rattlesnake jump out just in front of my donkey—and Mr. Du B enlivened the ride by telling us hunting stories and giving us scenes of cracker life. He told us a little story of a cracker's description of an umbrella. The cracker went acourting & among the rest of his intellectual converse said he "Sall, by golly did you ever seed an umberilla." "No, John, law du tell." "Well it's got a top for all the world like a May apple, it's as green as pizen & shoves up & down, oh golly! !" He also gave us a description of cracker speeches. At a Georgia election the two men up for office were Dr Black and a Mr. Zimmerman. The cracker was holding forth for Dr B. "Feller Citizens, whomsomever has hern tell of the naturalization of Mr. Zinemern's abiliters. But Dr Black has been to Philleme York and has larned to conspute and argufy on all subjects whatsumdever. He can cure the rappidamic. He gives his patients a little snake root and a little saxifac and puts him into a pestiferation, and cures him diabolically. Feller citizens, he's the chap." And occasionally Mr. P. in order to ridicule my genteel appearance would sing "If I had a donkey what couldn't go" or else would advise me to put my setting poles down and drive my ass along.

After riding twelve miles through a desolate country without seeing only one house we came to the capital of Nassau County, the emporium of fashion for Nassau County. The court house being the largest building I will describe first. It was a building 30 by 20 feet, a small two story building roughly boarded up, with neither ceiling or plastering, with two windows of glass & a half a dozen others with shutters. The jury rooms were close by, being enclosures of poles with board roofs about 15 feet wide. Beside the court house & jury rooms there are two cracker houses & these comprise the edifices belonging to the capital of Nassau County. We found about 150 cracker men & women on the ground dressed in their sparking rig & full of fun & humour. We here learned that Judge Bronson had sent word that he would not hold court here but would adjourn it until next spring. While here I heard a quarrel between the two candidates for the legislature from this county. Both contended that they were elected and both had certificates from the county clerk. The one was a very modest clever young lawyer, the other a noisy blustering man not devoid of talent but full of low abuse & vulgarity. He made a speech remarkable for its egotistical nonsense & high flown crackerisms. I never laughed more. It was so rich, so new, so unlike anything we have at the north. After loafing for two or three hours we returned. I here drank water worse than any mud hole in Adams. We rode back two miles to the house of a cracker, the only house on the road, & leaving my donkey to pick a thistle I took dinner, a regular cracker dinner, & "the way I walked into the provisions" as the crackers say "was mighty *curous.*" We returned home just at evening & spent the evening very pleasantly in social chit chat. Mr. Du B told us multitudes of negro anecdotes of the peculiar expressions of these negroes. The day has been exceedingly hot & I do not think I ever suffered so much with the heat in the world, altho my clothing was quite thin and there was a good breeze. The last day of November & suffering with heat! ! very unlike a northern winter truly.

December 1. Today we returned to St. Marys and right glad was I to get back, altho' such trips are very conducive to health. Mr. Du B has invited me to accompany him on a bear hunt in a few days and I think I shall go. Today we have another yellow day. I am very much amused with the southern peculiarities of expression. A southerner says for "I think" "I reckon," for "sun rise" "sun up," for "sun set" "sun down," for "carry" "tote," "right smart chance" for "a good opportunity," for "a great many," "a heap." "Ugly" is used entirely to express homeliness & there are thousands of these peculiar expressions which we notice each day. But the negro race have many more than any race I have ever seen. They abound in queer phrases and comical blunders—but of all the men I have ever seen a plantation hand beats all for clipping his words & using odd sayings. For a long time it was impossible for me to understand a word of what they said—and their singing was as unintelligible. It is a peculiar kind of idiom peculiar to themselves. Their fondness for high flown comparisons and large sounding words lead them into the most egregious and laughable blunders. The cracker population have a drawling way of speaking and use a great many words much like the backwoods population of North Carolina. It is a crackerism, not a specimen of the English language.

December 2ond 1843. I left St. Marys today in company with Mr. Preston of this place for Jacksonville, Duval County, E. Florida. We took the steamer Gaston and owing to the roughness of the sea we suffered somewhat with that awfully disagreeable feeling, sea sickness. Jacksonville is a very good specimen of a modern Florida town. Its citizens vainly imagine that Jacksonville is the ne plus ultra of civilization & refinement and that in them strangers can behold all that is desirable in mankind. The soil is exceedingly sandy and every step you take it seems as if you would sink beneath the sand. The houses are poorly constructed & the place is dull enough. There are some very talented and agreeable men who reside here, & were it not for these there would be no redeeming traits in its character. I remained at Jacksonville[9] four days and during that time saw quite enough of the place. While here I visited the plantation of Mr. Sadler and was much pleased with its order and general appearance. It is beautifully situated on the river St. Johns about five miles from

[9] Whipple's footnote: There once was an old verse
"Start a cow thief where you will
He'll bend his way to Jacksonville."

Jacksonville. He has quite a small village. Besides the plantation house & the overseer's house there are about 30 negro houses and the cotton houses &c &c. His crop is mainly cotton. He puts up this year about 100,000 pounds of the best sea island cotton besides raising sugar cane, corn & other grains. Mr. Sadler's management of his negroes is very good. While I was there he broke his driver. He had been detected in stealing peas and that only a week after 300 bushels had been distributed among the negroes. The fellow plead guilty & was flogged 75 lashes on the bare back and another appointed in his place. These negroes have to be kept in rather strict, yet Mr. Sadler's negroes are decidedly a happy set of negroes compared to many in the south. After spending the day at Mr. Sadler's we returned to Jacksonville in the evening. While here I heard of two more shooting scrapes in Florida. Horrible. I would not live in Florida, in many sections of it, for a mine of gold. For several days I have felt unhappy and I know not what to attribute it to except to my not having read my Bible so much of late. But henceforth I will not allow anything to come in between me and my duty to my God. I have witnessed twice within the last week most beautiful meteors and no one can imagine their beautiful and brilliant appearance. Sunset & sunrise are very beautiful here, indeed I have never witnessed such in any other section of the country. God has decked this southern land with many beauties and man, vile man, has made it the scene of corruption & blood. Oh may Almighty God watch over me lest I too fall into these heinous sins. We returned to St. Marys December 6th and found it as we left it like Goldsmith's deserted village. Have received a letter from Sarah & my father but none from my dear wife. God bless her & my child. My dear father urges me to pray "lead me not into temptation." May God hear that prayer & may I ever utter it wherever I go.

December 6th 1843 St. Marys, Georgia. Since writing the above I have thought it might be well for me to describe more fully the meteors I mentioned on the other page. The first was seen by me at about ½ past 11 P. M. at Mr. Du Buske's plantation, Nassau County, Florida. The sky was remarkably clear & the evening very light. The meteor seemed to start immediately over my head and descended rapidly to the horizon. It had a fiery red appearance and looked to be as large as a good sized wicket ball. When near the earth it exploded and the flash was like that of burning powder & it then presented a great variety of beautiful hues for the instant and then vanished. It was remarkably brilliant and unlike any I had seen before. This was the eve of 30 November. The other was seen on the eve of Dec 5th. It was more yellow in appearance and exploded in like manner. After the explosion it descended to the earth in two or three streams of fire, looking not unlike fire rockets in the act of explosion. The appearance of these meteors in such a brilliant night and their unusually beautiful appearance will long remain fresh in my memory.

The first frost of the season appeared yesterday eve on the St. Johns and vicinity, but it was so slight that it did not injure any plants. The weather is a little cooler, but is still much like our warm fall weather. Everything has the appearance of summer and old dame nature clings to her gay robes of green with a remarkable tenacity. I today met a very pleasant gentleman from Charleston, a very heavy dealer in cotton, and from him learned something new of the cotton crop. He says that the prospects for planters are poor. This must be the cry year after year under the operation of slavery. For the sons of the planter are generally reared in idleness & extravagance, so when he comes to act for himself he rushes madly in debt and too often his ruin is effected. The legitimate tendency of slavery is to make each generation more & more inefficient and less & less moral. To say nothing of slavery as it regards the black population, it is ruinous to the whites. Here & there you will find men who will rise to a standing in society in spite of froward circumstances but for the mass corruption will increase with each successive generation. The luxury & sloth of many southerners are well calculated to ruin & degrade all that is truly noble in character. A few men rise, but the mass fall still deeper and deeper in degradation & vice. But Florida is the tip of the top for rascality and knavery. Nowhere this side of Texas can you find so many rascals who live by their wits. One half of the population of most modern towns in Florida are ruined spendthrifts and too many of the balance are rogues & scoundrels.

The manner in which the Florida war was conducted as far as finances are concerned is unparalleled in history for knavery. Millions were extorted from the government upon false oaths and he who could excel in rascality was looked up to as a paragon of talent. Indeed one man, the son in law of one of these Florida claimants, told me "that he knew that men swore to things in reference to that claim as false as false could be." Indeed, now I believe there are many men in Florida who would swear hell was heaven & crime virtue if thereby their ends could be effected. The lawyers received 10 per cent for their fees and that acted as a salve to their consciences, for with them too often money is held superior to honor & virtue. Their fees were enormous and what cared they for the right or wrong of the claims. $5000, $7000,

$10,000, $15,000 were paid as attorney fees in prosecuting these claims. Wood was sold to the army at $10 per cord in the woods and since the close of the war, they are continually bringing in claims for loss of houses, for rations & for pay. 20 millions will not pay all the cost of this Florida War & the McIntosh rebellion. Honour, virtue & religion have had to flee before rascality, crime & selfishness. But it is to be hoped that a new day will yet dawn on Florida and that its new settlers will bring with them peace & virtue. The legislature of Florida was but a few years since a pandemonium, and some of the members were so very ignorant they could neither read or write. Any person travelling either in Georgia or Florida would not wonder that English writers laugh at the profusion of military titles in America. Every man has a title and I believe the Romans themselves could not boast of more military men or rather men bearing military titles.

December 12, 1843 The more intimately I become acquainted with southern men and the peculiar institutions of the south the more do I notice their peculiarities. The southerner himself is different from the northerner in many striking particulars. He is more chivalrous, that is to say, he has more of that old English feeling common in the days of the feudal system & crusades. He is liberal in his feelings, high minded, a warm & generous friend but a malignant and bitter enemy. He forms his attachments easier and does not retain them as long as men of a less ardent disposition. He is generous to a fault with his property, is fond of gaiety and pleasure & generally dislikes the routine of business. His habits are those of genteel idleness or of the man of leisure. Nothing is a too expensive gratification of appetite or feeling, which his purse will permit him to buy. There are some gentlemen however that I have met who differ in very many particulars from the above description and whose habits of life are those of a prudent & careful business man. But these I may say are the exceptions. It is unfortunate that in a country where menial labour is performed entirely by slaves, that there industry is generally looked upon if not dishonorable, at least as of doubtful gentility. It is a matter of deep regret that talent & genius is often buried forever, by this blind following the impulses of a life of pleasure. These false principles instilled into the minds of children if not by precept, by every day practice often serve as a lure to lead them to destruction. The luxurious habits of southerners is ruinous in the extreme and it has resulted in the embarrassment and ruin of many planters. Prudence and the most rigid habits of economy can alone retrieve the almost ruined fortunes of the south. The evil is a great one and it is this luxurious mode of living, with reckless expenditure, that has & ever will prevent the prosperity of the southern states.

The laws of the slave states are severe for the free black population. They are infinitely better off as slaves than as free men. But there is not a more ignorant & debased white population in the United States than the lower class of whites in Georgia. And it is from the fact of the numbers of these men on juries, that all legal questions which go to juries are deemed not more certain than the throw of the dice. A gentleman of this place (St. Marys) the Rev. Mr. Baird related to me a curious fact of the utter ignorance of these backwoods cracker juries. A man in Wayne County was arrested for stealing a broadaxe. The fact was clearly proved and the jury after deliberating several hours brought in a verdict of *murder* in the first degree. The judge reprimanded them and sent them back and after deliberating for some time they came back into court and very gravely told the judge they could not make it anything else. There are many similar transactions altho' not as bad that have been related to me as specimens of the ignorance of the poor class of whites. The fact that all menial labour is performed by slaves causes this class of the southern population to be despised by all. I had rather be a well treated slave than one of the low & poor whites. Dr Judson related to me today a case where a jury manifestly decided a case not only wrong, but in violation of all law & equity. Nightingale vs. a sea captain. The facts were these, after the captain had left the port of St. Marys 8 or 9 days bound for Maine he found a slave had stowed himself away in the hold. The law of Georgia orders that in such a case he should put back into port. But he could not do this and proceeded to Maine, where the slave went to Canada. The master commenced a suit for the slave value & for abducting him. It was settled by the Captain's giving his bond for the delivery of the negro back to the master within a certain time. The master accompanied the Captain to Canada & through some means decoyed the negro back on this side the lines & he was there arrested. The captain after coming with the negro there made a formal delivery in the presence of witnesses of the negro to the master, who accepted him. But the master, desiring to make a show of his kind treatment and also show how foolishly slaves ran away & how glad they were to come back, kept him about him at the Astor house as his servant, but soon the negro again ran away and stole all he could lay his hands on. The master could not find him and after returning here sued the captain & recovered $900 judgt.

There is no court of appeals in Georgia & of course there is but little certainty of right & justice being properly meted

out to those who engage in law. The judge has great power &
can exercise a great influence over such men as are found on
petit juries. Mrs. Reid told me of an amusing revenge the
"crackers" had on her husband by sending him to Congress
to get rid of him as judge. Judge Reid was once taken all
aback, as the sailors say, after performing the ceremony of
marrying two of these crackers, the man ugly enough but
the woman beyond all comparison for hideousness. Says
Judge R "now kiss her, you are one." "Arter your honor
is manners," said the cracker, causing members of the
bar present to shout with laughter. The Rev. Mr. Baird related to me a very humorous story of one of these backwoods
crackers who received a love letter from his inamorata &
the question was how he could learn its contents and not
have any one else know it, as he could not read, so he went
to one of his neighbors who could read and made an arrangement that he should read it aloud & the cracker should
stand behind him and stop his ears so that the reader could
not hear it. Mr. Bacon of this place, speaking of some members of the legislature of Georgia, said that they only needed
long ears and a tail to have their classification among beasts
distinctly marked out.

Dec 16, 1843 At the invitation of Rev. Mr. Baird & Mr.
Griswold I accompanied them today on a visit to the plantation of Col. Hallows, a half pay officer in the New Grenada
service who served under Bolivar in the Columbian war. We
found his place a beautiful one situated in a fine grove of
large hickory trees & were cordially welcomed. Our ride lay
through pine barrens & oak shrub for seven miles and the ride
would have been excessively dull had it not been enlivened
by humorous anecdotes by Mr. Baird of a speech made by a

cracker in legislature against steam doctors, of a cracker woman's testimony &c &c. He is very facetious and quite witty. Col. Hallows raises sugar cane & cotton in small quantities but his principal crop was arrow root this year. He puts up about 3000lb for which he will receive about 30 cts. per lb. The manner of its preparation for market is very interesting. The outer skin is first removed, then it is thoroughly washed, then it is grated fine, then again washed & squeezed through fine sieves and then dried and packed. I have never spent a pleasanter day away from home. Mrs. Hallows is a very pleasant and intelligent lady and a paragon of industry. We spent the morning very pleasantly in viewing his grounds & plantation and after dinner returned to St. Marys, all of us delighted with our visit. I saw roses blooming today in his garden & we had fine oranges for our dessert. The day was quite warm and grateful after the cold rain storm of the last few days.

Dec 17, & 18 Extremely warm, thermometer stands at 75 in the shade. I saw a great variety of roses and other flowers in full bloom today in the garden.

Dec 20 Spent this evening at Mr. Sadlers at a candy party and employed myself very pleasantly. Mr. Sadler gave me some laughable accounts of the extreme superstition and ignorance of the negroes. The negroes have a curious way of curing the elongation of the palate by pulling their hair, and also of the surprise of one of his negroes when he first saw a rice mill and of another who saw canal locks. After listening to some sweet music on the piano from Miss S & partaking of the hospitality of this excellent family we returned much gratified with our visit.

Dec 21. I visited today the ship Tecumseh Capt. Ripley bound for St. Iago[10] freighted with lumber and had a very pleasant visit. Capt. Ripley is a devoted Christian and has family prayers morning and evening on ship board. He says he has always found that his own business prospers by attending strictly to that of his master Jesus. His wife and daughter are with him. Their cabin is pleasantly furnished & has a piano & a small library. I was much gratified with my visit and wish all sea captains loved the Saviour as much as Capt. Ripley does. The weather is warm and oppressive.

Dec 25. Christmas day. At 12 o'clock we were all aroused from a sound sleep by the music of the negroes commencing the celebration of the Christmas holidays. A more motley group of dark skins I have never seen, all arrayed in their holiday dresses and full of joy and gladness at the return of their annual holidays. Their masters give them their time at this season of the year to celebrate the holidays and none can imagine the joy & enthusiasm with which a slave hails these seasons of festive enjoyment. As soon as we were up the servants were all waiting with laughing faces to wish us a Merry Christmas, expecting to receive a bit or so as a contribution. I was truly gratified at the joyous faces of the negroes who met me in the street and their cheerful "happy Christmas, massa" made me feel a part of their happiness in hailing the Christmas holidays. In company with Mr. Hill & Griswold I left Saint Marys to visit the plantation of Genl Clinch, who resides about 27 miles from here upon the Satilla River.[11] Our

[10] Probably Santiago, Cuba.

[11] Brigadier General Duncan L. Clinch (1787–1849) entered the regular army in 1808. He served through the War of 1812, in 1815 was assigned to the Fourth Infantry, and was made colonel in 1819. He probably acquired his property in Georgia during these years, for he was stationed in that state and in North Carolina much of the time. At about the same time he was promoted to a colonelcy he was

route lay through the pine barrens so common in the low country of Georgia. And we were astonished at the extreme sparseness of the population. We rode 23 miles only seeing 3 houses on our route and over as fine roads as I have ever seen. The road is dull and monotonous, as it is but one continual succession of pine trees thinly scattered over immense plains with no underbrush, and here and there we found small patches of swamp and hammock lands. We reached the residence of the Hero of Withlacochie residence just before dinner and were cordially welcomed. After partaking of an excellent Christmas dinner and enjoying a quiet siesta of an hour or so we took a walk out over his plantation. Genl Clinch has one of the largest rice plantations in this section of country. He plants about 500 acres and has over one hundred field hands. The land is of the richest alluvial soil and owing to the deposits made upon it by the influx of the tide is inexhaustible. The land is surrounded by large embankments and laid out in squares of about 15 or 20 acres each, these intersected by ditches & embankments with flood gates to flow the land or to drain it so that one plot can be overflowed and another dry at the same time. The crop is planted in February and ripens about the last of August. After planting, the land is flowed until time for hoeing, then drained & hoed & then flowed again. The flowing of the land is beneficial in keep-

put in command of the Eastern Division, Seventh Military District, with his headquarters first at Fernandino, Florida, and then at St. Marys, Georgia. Subsequently he was brevetted brigadier general and spent some time at Baton Rouge and at Jefferson Barracks, Missouri, as well as at Mobile. At the outbreak of the second Seminole War he was in command in Florida but resigned in 1836 on account of the attitude of the War Department. From then until the time of his death he resided on his plantation near St. Marys, except for a short period in 1844–45, when he ran for Congress to fill an unexpired term, was elected, and served to the end of that Congress in March, 1845. See Fred. Cubberly, "Fort King," *Florida Historical Society Quarterly*, 5:139 ff., for several references to Clinch in the Seminole War.

ing down grass and weeds besides enriching the land. This land is worth from $100 to $200 per acre. It costs about 75 dollars to clear it and put into an excellent state of cultivation. After reaping it is threshed with a machine or flail, then winnowed and finally divested of the rough hull by means of mortars and pestles. Genl Clinch raised this year about 25,000 bushels, which brings him about 60c per bushel. He raises about 70 bushels to the acre and its weight is about 46^lb to the bushel. Genl Clinch is a good master and follows the task system. I found his daughters pleasant and agreeable as well as accomplished ladies. Here I found the negroes enjoying the holidays to the fill. Dancing was to be heard & seen from early dawn to 11 & 12 o'clock at night. The tamborine and fiddle were in constant use and the General's piazza in front of his house was used as the ball room. The negroes are good dancers and I laughed heartily at the quaint expressions & blunders of these negroes. They vie with each other in attentions to the fair sex and delight above all to ape the manners of the whites. I heard some fine negro songs a few lines of which I caught & insert. "Laugh you nigger, laugh away. Laugh, you chile 'tis holiday. Dance, you cuffy, dance away. 'Tis Christmas holiday. Sing, boys, sing sing away, sing for 'tis de holiday. Roll your eye, show your teeth, fiddle & dance away, 'tis holiday."

We spent the next day there and left after dinner & delighted with our visit. Long shall I remember the Christmas holidays in Georgia. I saw roses the 26th December in bloom in Genl Clinch's garden. The weather is quite warm, almost sultry. We reached Saint Marys about 10½ P.M. fatigued with our long ride through the woods of Georgia.

Dec 27. This is with the negroes the last day of the feast and with them the "great day." The negroes are out in great numbers arrayed in their best and their ebony faces shine with joy and happiness. Already have they paraded, with a corps of staff officers with red sashes, mock epaulettes & goose quill feathers, and a band of music composed of 3 fiddles, 1 tenor & 1 bass drum, 2 triangles & 2 tamborines and they are marching up & down the streets in great style. They are followed by others, some dancing, some walking & some hopping, others singing, all as lively as lively can be. If any negro refuses to join them they seize him & have a mock trial & sentence him to a flogging which is well laid on. Already have they had several such court martials. Here they come again with flags flying and music enough to deafen one & they have now two fifes to increase their noise. Whatever others may think, I am satisfied that these seasons of joyous mirth have a happy effect upon the negro population. They levy contributions on all the whites they see & thus find themselves in pocket money. I am really sore I have laughed so long and so heartily. Every negro's face is wreathed in smiles & never have I seen such a display of ebony & ivory in my life and never expect to again. Mr. Sadler gave me an interesting account today of the proceedings of the blacks on his plantation during the holidays and of the way in which he cured his negroes of fighting. These scenes of joyous mirth are like manna to a hungry soul to these fun loving Africans and the effect must be good. It would make a northern abolitionist change his sentiments in reference to slavery could he see as I have seen the jollity & mirth of the black population during the Christmas holidays. Never have I seen any class of people who appeared to enjoy more than do these negroes. And during my visit to the plantation of Genl C I was gratified by the kind feeling which seemed to exist between the master and his slave. On the breaking up of the dance each slave came in and bade his "massa good night" and all seemed to feel as if he were their dearest and best friend. There was none of that fear, that servile fear, that is the offspring of tyranny and cruelty. I know there are men who do not treat their slaves kindly, men whose slaves bear the looks of abject sorrow but these are the exceptions not the general rule.

Dec 28th The political character of Georgia is very wavering and with no certainty can you form an opinion of the result of an election. Local feelings and personal preferences are more often called out in opposition to attachment to party than among the intelligent northern states. The educated Georgians are as strong for ought I know in their political preferences as are any members of the parties at the north, but the backwoods people are easily gulled and made the dupes of for the benefit of designing men, and when they have once made up their mind about a man or a measure no argument can change them. This gives to Georgia elections the character of a drama. The scenes are constantly shifting. The party in power today may be in the minority tomorrow. General Clinch is the candidate of the Whig party for member of Congress in the place of Mellen deceased and I think will be elected. The Hero of Withlacochie is as popular in the low country of Georgia as the Hero of North Bend[12] was in Ohio. All love him for his courage, for his energy of character, for his talents & for his kindness of heart. I am inclined to think that the Democratic party of Georgia is stronger than most think it is on the question for the next presidency. Martin Van Buren has many warm and true hearted friends among

[12] William Henry Harrison.

the Democracy of Georgia & they feel a generous pride in upholding New York's favorite son.

This evening received a call from Mr. Sadler and while quietly enjoying ourselves in social chit chat we were all startled by a loud knocking at the door and our room was soon filled by a company of masquers, men in petticoats, turbans, false faces &c &c. It was really one of the most grotesque appearances I have seen since I came south. The several parts were well executed and we were all highly entertained. After entertaining us for some half hour or so they departed to visit others. This is one way in which the holidays are kept south.

In many places masquerading is very fashionable at this season of the year and much humour is sometimes displayed in the arrangement. All kinds of laughable and fantastic disguises are used and sometimes they are productive of great merriment.

Dec 29 As we (Mr. Hill & myself) intend leaving St. Marys tomorrow I have spent this day in making farewell visits. I have formed some very pleasant acquaintances here and some friends who will ever be esteemed by me until life shall close. Among them are first Mr. Sadler & family & Mr. J. Preston & family. Long shall I remember their kind attentions and their hospitality. Mr. Sadler's family is such as you will find few to equal it in the south. I spent the evening there this evening and regretted much to leave this estimable family & bid them farewell. May they & all other friends & relatives altho obliged to be sundered in this world be united in a world of eternal joy above. Farewell—to St. Marys and to its inhabitants. It is ever thus. No sooner are we bound to any portion of the human race by a pleasing acquaintance than we are obliged to whisper that chilling sound, farewell.

December 30th 1843 This morning I bade adieu to St. Marys and to the kind friends I have here met and really felt quite melancholy at bidding adieu even to the friends who were strangers to me but yesterday. Thus it is in this transitory & fleeting world. We form friendships today which are sundered tomorrow. We are all floating on the stream of time, towards an eternity. We meet on our course and tomorrow perhaps are parted forever. Farewell, dear friends, a long farewell, yet in memory will your kindness ever be as fresh as it is today. Mr. Hill & myself took the steamer Wm Gaston & came to Picolata, stopping a few hours at Jacksonville, that city of Florida described before. The scenery on the St. Johns is delightful and romantic. This river is from ¾ to 3 miles wide and its shores are scolloped here and there with numerous small bays and inlets which add beauty to the scene. The tide rises and falls for a great distance on this river & the country around it is very level & the land is in many places very fertile. Here & there we saw beautiful groves of wild oranges & occasionally were amused by watching some sleepy alligator. We arrived at Picolata about 7 o'clock in the evening & were amused by the solitary & lonesome looking place emblem of Dicken's Eden. Here we took the stage and after a five hours ride over 18 miles of Florida woods we reached St. Augustine. As it was very late I put up at the Florida House, a miserable hotel by the way, and remained there over the Sabbath. Sunday evening I visited the graveyard where the remains of the gallant officers who perished during the Florida War are buried. Here lies the bones of Lieut. H. Wardwell, an early friend of mine. Poor fellow, he like hundreds of others full of ambitious hopes & joyous expectations met an early grave.

January 1, 1844 "A new year." *True* a year has gone into an eternity and for its opportunities of doing good I shall have to give an a/c at the bar of God. May this year be indeed a new year. May it be spent more for God & less for this world. Oh! may it be indeed a happy new year made so by the presence of a Saviour's smiles. I always feel melancholy at the end of a year when I think of the wasted time, of the lost opportunities of doing good. The day is delightfully warm and pleasant, very unlike our new year's days at the north. The day is not observed much here by calling but there are a few who still keep up the old Knickerbocker custom of calling. There is to be a large ball this evening but as I am unacquainted with the givers of it I am not of the invited guests. Besides, these midnight scenes of fashion would not be very beneficent to my health. I understand there are to be a party of masquers there. The party of masquers at this ball are to be arrayed as Indians and will dance the war dance of the Seminoles. I would like to see a scene like this but on the whole I am happy to avoid this as well as all such scenes of festive mirth as it always produces an unhappy effect upon my health. I have formed several very pleasant acquaintances since I returned. Among them are Dr Balwin of New York and Mr. Peck of the firm of Peck and Layne. Mr. Peck has been largely engaged in merchandise in Florida & has amassed a large property.

January 4, 1843. [*sic*] Today in the company of Lieut. Benham & a large party of gentlemen & ladies we visited the old Spanish fort at this place & I gave it a more thorough examination than before. It was built during the reign of Isabella or near that time, for [it was] over one hundred years since the northern bastion was rebuilt as it had then been so long built that it was going to decay. It resembles the plan below very much and has a ditch around it.[13] The fort proper is about 300 feet long & about 250 feet in breadth. The fort & outer works cover an area of about five acres. It is built of soft shell stone which is found here in great abundance and it is said to answer much better than stone of a harder nature, as the ball at once lodges in the wall & does not injure the fortification but rather serves to strengthen it. The three dungeons in the northeast corner were only discovered about 8 or 10 years since and in the farther one was found the bones of a man. The poor fellow may have died a victim to Spanish cruelty. These dungeons are the most dismal character & seem to have been invented solely for purposes of cruelty. They may have been used at one time as the rooms of the bloody inquisition. There was undoubtedly at one time a draw bridge at the entrance and the embankment in front of the gate in the shape of a half moon was in order to protect the entrance of the fort from cannon of the enemy. Upon this embankment is a coat of arms and this part of it appears to have once been an altar. The old chapel is in a good state of repair. The altar is perfect as also two niches where doubtless were images placed for worship. In one of the rooms is a very large mahogany chest 8 feet long by 4 feet high & 4 feet wide made of mahogany and having heavy iron bands enclosing it. In another apartment is a pair of immense gun wheels made of mahogany. Doubtless at that time mahogany was supposed to be one of the most durable kinds of wood.

[13] The manuscript has a pen diagram at the foot of the page with explanatory data.

So much did this fort cost that it is said the King vainly thought it must have been built in part of gold.

Masquerading is very common here at this season of year. They commence masquing during the Christmas holidays & continue it until Lent. This custom appears to have grown out of the old Spanish manner of keeping carnival. These masquers select their own disguises and then visit from house to house acting their several parts. At times these disguises & the acting is excellent but many times it resembles the fantastics seen on militia training days. Sometimes the masquers send word to a gentleman that they will dance at his house in the evening and he provides the entertainment and they take their music with them and after having acted their several parts they don their disguises & spend the evening in social chit chat. This, as well as all other old Spanish customs, is fast disappearing and they are giving way to American tastes & American amusements, much to the benefit of morality. The Catholic Church seldom interferes in the pleasures of its followers even if they are of a doubtful nature & will not check them unless they have become the direct means of promoting crime. This is ever the case with a religion based upon the superstition of its people. On the contrary, a pure religion aims at cleansing all the fountains of pleasure as well as to cure the open evils of the community.

Today while walking on the sea wall commonly called the "lovers walk" I observed a curious animal, neither fish, flesh nor fowl but which seemed possessed of animal life. It was of a globular form & apparently an entirely muscular substance. Daily do I meet new things & see sights which remind me I am away from my northern home. Yet notwithstanding all its charms & pleasures all is stale & devoid of happiness when my wife is away & cannot share these joys with me.

This evening we had three companies of masquers at Mrs. Reid's. The first was a company of three Minorcan girls disguised as old women. They dance beautifully. The acting was done to the life. The second company were dressed as a hideous old man and a would be fashionable woman—and the third company consisted of a barber, his sweetheart, a homely black woman, a little decrepit old man. They brought their tamborine & violin with them and for about a half an hour we had as lively a dance as was ever seen. Every evening there are several parties of these masquers who go from house to house. This will be kept up until Lent. The three days before Lent are kept as a carnival & then these parties of masquers may be seen at all hours parading the streets and visiting from house to house. There was a large party of masquers out last evening of "the elite" of the town. The Hon. Mrs. Bronson disguised as an Indian squaw, Lieut. Runford as Billy Bowlegs, Miss Spafford as an old Irish woman & Lieut. Lee as her son, Miss Hernandez, Miss Worth & Miss Humphreys as nuns. The disguises and acting were said to be excellent altho' it is very doubtful whether this kind of amusement well suited the dignity and standing of some of the parties concerned. It is certain it would be deemed a letting down of dignity among our northern people, but among the Romans some do as the Romans do.

January 5th This evening we were highly entertained by the acting of three masquers who came here twice & spent some half hour each time. The man Mr. Benet was disguised as a deaf and dumb man and he acted his part well. By no trick of calling him suddenly or holloaing in his ear could you make him show that he heard you. Miss Seque was disguised as an old country woman & she acted her part admirably & Miss Benet appeared as her daughter Kate. She was taking the benefit of leap year and was seeking a husband for Kate. She amused us well by her description of her daughter and Miss Benet acted the part of a simple country girl admirably. They made a dancing party and danced & waltzed for our amusement. We were unable to penetrate their disguises and would not have known them but for their letting the secret out as they left. It was a capital masquerade & we were all highly pleased with the acting.

January 6, 1843 [*sic*] In company with a large party of 23 ladies and gentlemen I today visited the quarries of conchina which are near this place. We left here in four row boats and had a spirited race over from the landing place. We went about two miles to the quarry which is now being used. This shell is of a very singular formation and is here found in immense quantities. There are quarries here which have doubtless been opened more than 100 years, indeed doubtless the stone for the old Spanish fort was procured here. Perhaps here in these quarries Indian slaves worked under Spanish task masters. After rambling about here for an hour or more we walked through a small piece of brush land to the beach & here we had a fine ramble along the old ocean shore for a mile or two & then we returned to the landing place, where our negroes had a fine collation prepared for us, and I assure my friends I for one had a sharp appetite after a six miles ramble through Florida sand. I noticed the passion vine wild, the cactus, the myrtle & several other plants which are culti-vated at the north. The day was delightfully warm and pleasant & we all enjoyed it much. In the evening after our return we were all again entertained by two companies of masquers, who kept us laughing while we remained. Gov.

Duval gave us some fine stories during the evening of his exploits &c &c. "Kicking his neighbor out of bed" "stealing his bed" &c &c. Weighed myself today & found I weighed 155lb, which is a gain of 11lb since I left home, which shows a southern clime agrees very well with me.

"Take no thought of the morrow" appears to be the motto of very many of the southern population altho' not in a scriptural sense. Instead of being sure they are right & then going ahead very many "go ahead" and then find to their sorrow they are wrong. The energies of the south under the present state of society are not called forth to great and noble purposes. They either lie dormant in idleness & luxury or receive a wrong direction and are expended in visionary projects or in reckless expenditures for useless luxuries & foolish dissipation. Without doubt the south has had & still has an immense amount of talent which lies & will continue to lie dormant entirely unproductive. This state of things is ruinous to any country no matter how much chivalry & generosity it may contain. A southern man is educated in nine cases out of ten to be a gentleman, an unproductive gentleman, a term which sometimes means a helpless being who is dependent on others for even the smallest offices of labor. There are exceptions, many of them, but even the large number of these does not alter the universality of the rule. Better far for our country if these were the mass & the others the exceptions.

I had an old house pointed out to me today which some aver is the identical house once occupied by the overseer who built the fort at this place. If so it is indeed a relic which should be kept for its past history. St. Augustine is full of these old rat castles & dismal houses only fit for owl nests which tell us of other days when this part of our country was under the dominion of the Spanish, and I love to wander through these narrow streets and stop to gaze upon these monitors of time, which whisper to us that the hands who built them are long since mouldering in the tomb.

As an evidence of the difference between slave & free labor Mrs. Reid has seven boarders & one child in her family, making eight & one persons. She keeps 1 cook, 1 chamber maid, 1 man servant, 1 little girl, 1 washerwoman—5 persons to do the work of nine, & not unfrequently you will see a servant for every member of the household. This work would all be done by one or two servants at the north. Such is the sloth & luxury of the mass of whites in the south.

January 9 Today I had a fine sail down the bay to the north beach and lagoon east of the light house. The wind blew very fresh and we dashed along the bay quite merrily. Our sail boat was one of these cypress canoes so extremely lottish [*sic*] that one must not change sides of a quid of tobacco, and at one time I expected we should be ducked, while we were just in the edge of the breakers. The waves ran so high that at times we were down out of sight under the wave in the trough of the sea. Here we rambled about two or three hours looking up shells &c &c. I found a few of the more common sort, some of which were quite pretty. I love dearly to ramble over the beach & see wave after wave come dashing over the sandy shore.

This evening we were highly entertained with the masquers who visited us. We had three parties. The two first were rather common altho the disguises were very good, but the third was capital. Mr. Marine was dressed as a Spanish brigand with a carbine, pistols, dirks & bowie knife & was really one of the most hideous figures I ever saw. His sister was dressed as his wife and had a malicious gipsy look, &

her long black hair streaming over her neck made her look beautiful. She had a guitar strung on her shoulder. A younger sister was disguised as the daughter and was well dressed and pretty. They spoke very rapidly in Spanish & the ladies acted their part admirably in stealing hdkfs, purses &c &c. They closed by singing "the brigands' song" in Spanish. The remainder of the party were dressed one as a negro, one as an alderman, wealthy, blustering & drinking, one as a flower girl &c &c. Every one seems to have entered into the spirit of masquing this year & no wonder, the example having been set by the daughters of Genl Worth & Genl Hernandez, Mrs. Bronson & others who call themselves the elite of the place. Certainly it appears to me to be a doubtful manner of amusement for an accomplished lady.

January 10. I have been thinking for some days that I would enter in my note book a few of the items of expenditure during the Florida war. The expenses of the war are said to have been between 20,000,000 and 25,000,000 of dollars, this besides the claims for losses &c &c. Never have I heard of such recklessness in the purchase of the needful supplies for troops. In one case 40 cords of wood is said to have cost the government $7,000 and this wood was landed in the woods. Steamboats which were not worth more than 10,000 or 15,000 dollars rented for 300 dollars per day. Negroes were hired at $40 per month & found & guaranteed to the master against being killed by the Indians. One company of men stationed at Mandarin it is said cost the government nearly $50 per month for each man & with a few exceptions all these volunteer companies were of no benefit. A body of 1500 volunteers it is said cost the government $18,000,000 for less than a years service. At the close of the war pay was granted to companies which never existed only in imagination. Hay was purchased at enormous rates of $80 to $150 per ton. Provisions & stores of all kinds were bought at nearly as high prices as if they were made of some of the less valuable metals. And all this, mind, to expatriate the poor Seminole. To drive him from the graves of his fathers & from his pleasant hunting grounds. Treachery & deceit would not fully answer the purpose of driving him from his land and an ignominious war must be waged to carry out the wishes of those who were no better than the oppressors of the Indian. May not our nation tremble in view of some of her treatment towards the poor red men of the forest. Christianity loses its lovely appearance when exhibited to the barbarian in garments of blood. Well did Osceola say when shown his portrait "Good, but where is the white man's *'white flag.'*" It sickens one to follow the details of this Florida war, both the treachery & deceit and the extravagance and corruption of those who furnished supplies to the army.

January 12, 1844 I spent this evening at Mrs. Peck's, where a small party of 25 or 30 persons were invited and was much entertained. We had two masquing parties there & the parts were capitally acted. The first was admirable. Mr. Fareira was painted and dressed as a Seminole warrior, & he danced the war dance, going through with all the acting, whooping & the war whoop. It was so well done that it sent a thrill of terror through me that made me tremble. Then followed a double man, flower girls, pages, peasants, old women &c &c. They joined in a dance & then left. The other party had a Paul Pry, a Frenchman, a fruit woman, an old niggar with a banjo, a page, a quaker & a drunkard. I never have seen any disguises more perfect than these. Really this old Spanish town has much that interests & amuses the stranger. Not only is it renowned for its age & old appearance, but it is the only place where these old Spanish customs are kept up. Every evening we are entertained with a masquing party and no doubt we shall be thus amused until Lent.

Sunday Jan 14, 1844 Last Wednesday, the officers & some of the citizens had a gay picnic party over on the island to which I was invited but owing to indisposition I did not go. A Miss Drysdale of this city, a beautiful and accomplished young lady, made one of the gay party. While there she was quite indisposed & they did not return until 11 o'clock at night. Since then she has been dangerously ill and today is said to be dying. Never have I seen a greater gloom spread over the gay faces of a city than today. Mr. Rutledge, our estimable minister of the Episcopal Church, was in tears when he entered & seemed deeply affected. At the words in the Litany "In the hour of death" he fell as if dead & the service was closed. He is much better now—but for a time life seemed extinct. Only last Sabbath Mr. Rutledge preached a sermon to young & old warning them to be ready. Miss Drysdale is a communicant of the Episcopal Church & has a hope of eternal life through faith in Jesus Christ. Last evening she sent for a young man of this place to whom she had been long attached to bid him a long, a last farewell. Truly in the midst of life we are in death. May God in his mercy sanctify this afflicting dispensation of his providence to all of the gay & thoughtless society of this city. And oh may we all remember that in time we must prepare for eternity and be also ready, for we know not in what hour death will summon us to try the realities of an eternity. Her funeral was attended on Monday 15th by a very large number of the citizens. Eight of her intimates (young ladies) acted as pall bearers and very many of the friends of the deceased went as mourners. I have never witnessed a more solemn funeral. All seemed to be affected by the inroad which death had made upon the gay circle of this city. Her family are deeply afflicted and one of the boys, her brother, could hardly be torn away from the grave. Young Humphreys, the young man to whom she was engaged, looks like a shadow, so much has he altered in the last few days.

January 16. I visited the sugar plantation of Col. Hanson & was much pleased with the process of sugar making. The cane is ground through heavy rollers, thus pressing all the juice from the stalk. The juice of the cane is a little sweeter than rich sap of the maple at the north. The process of boiling is very similar to that of making maple sugar. The crop of cane resembles very much a field of corn. The cane is planted in January here & allowed to stand until the first frost, which is generally in November. The cane exhausts the land very rapidly and therefore lands for sugar planting should be of the richest character. 1200lb sugar is a fair crop to the acre. The weather has been exceedingly warm for the last few days, very much like our June weather at the north, thermometer at 80°. It is the boast of Floridians that there is never a day when you cannot see the sun. Whether this be true or not, I am sure there is but few days in the year when they do not have the benefit of its genial warmth. The gardens are well stocked with vegetables and nature wears the appearance of summer at the north. I saw a turnip yesterday (English) which weighed 13lb and measured 3 feet in circumference. If the people here were disposed to be industrious they would need but little labour to obtain a competence in this climate.

But slavery & a warm climate seem to have used up all energy & industry.

I heard today of a novel way of raising the wind, by creating a mineral spring & puffing it so as to attract invalids to it as a watering place. The formation of the earth is such in this part of the south that but few springs possessing mineral qualities are found. A Maj. Taylor somewhat celebrated for the peculiar qualifications of some Floridians sent to Charleston for a cask of saltpetre, a cask of sulphur, a cask of salts and had a mixture of the three deposited in a spring near his house & sent the water abroad for analysis and so puffed it that it became quite celebrated. After a time he became careless in the mixing of the quantities & the secret leaked out. I have been told a good story of a man's will being made after his death. All kinds of ingenious rascality seem to have been perpetrated at some time or other in Florida & one would almost believe that Florida could equal Texas in such interesting specimens of civilization.

January 18 The weather has again changed from very warm to exceedingly cool weather. The thermometer shows a change of 50 degrees in 40 hours. But as this kind of weather lasts but a short time in Florida one must have patience.

January 20 Today I listened to a beautiful sermon from the Rev. Mr. Rutledge on the death of Miss Drysdale. He was very eloquent and did justice to the subject. The house was very solemn & all seemed to feel in some slight degree the nothingness of life. Her family who were present seemed bowed down under the severe loss which they have sustained. Death is ever terrible but how much more so in the spring time of youth amid loved friends & coming suddenly and in an unexpected manner.

"Home sweet home, be it ever so humble there is no place like home." Never have I had such a flood of sweet memories roll over my mind as when these old time worn words appeared to me today. Oh! how full of meaning that one word "home." All men love home. Even the dumb brute shows delight at returning to his home. But how is that word hallowed when around that distant home is encircled all that can make life happy. How sweet are the recollections of that home when memory brings up with it all the familiar associations of childhood as well as the connections of later years, and how much sweeter still is the memory of that distant home when it is hallowed by the presence of a beloved wife and a smiling babe. Daily I meet with novelties, with curiosities. Life here may have to some charms infinitely beyond that of our colder clime, but if I would be happy give me my home, give me my loved ones around me, and then and only then can I enjoy that bliss which all seek for & few find. The old ruin, the vine clad wall, the sunny sky, the evergreen landscape have no charm for me when separated afar from those I love. The faces of strangers, the diversity of scenes, the old ruined houses & time worn walls only cause my mind to wander back to other & to happier days spent amid loved ones at my home.

January 21, 1844 Mrs. Reid gave me a good insight into a certain kind of Georgia character by describing the exploits of a young Georgian who made her a visit a few years since. The end and aim of his existence appeared to be to perpetrate some wicked joke upon others for his own amusement. At tea one evening they had hot buttered warfles. The Georgian did the honors of the table and after he had passed the warfles to all the rest, he offered them to his sister, but suddenly drawing back the plate with an elongated face he said in a whining voice, "I'm afraid to give Laura a "warfle." "Why so" asked the others. "Why" says he "you see Laura & I once went to a ball & you see they had hot buttered warfles & Laura ate & ate until I thought she was going to kill herself and when the warfles were passed around the last time don't you think she put a buttered warfle in her bag." When it was time to go we found Laura had left her bag & said she "do dear brother go & get, do get it now, won't you." "Why," said I, "I can get it just as well tomorrow. Is there anything in it you are in pressing need of?" "Oh! yes there is. I do want it very much for W^m, it's got a warfle in it." The poor girl burst into tears & left the table. There are many of these wicked wits south as well as north who are bent on having a joke even at the expense of the dearest friend. A specimen of the same kind of cruelty, I saw today perpetrated upon my friend Hill by a lady[14]—which made him miserable & did not add to the happiness of she who thus forgot her dignity and acted as his tormentor. True politeness after all seeks for the happiness of others and is not tied down by convention forms & pleasant nothings. May I never forget what is due to the feelings of others so much as to knowingly & wilfully trample on the feelings of others for the sake of enjoying a laugh at their expense. I never have met a lady who is possessed of true gentility in a greater degree than is Hon. Mrs. Reid and I shall long remember her not only as a kindhearted but also as a genteel and accomplished lady.

I have witnessed since I came south several slave sales and

---

[14] A footnote at the bottom of the page probably giving the name of the lady has been torn away.

have until today neglected to mention it. A slave auction is to me a melancholy sight. The pitiful faces of those to be sold, the jokes & witticisms heard on all sides, the indecent remarks which one is obliged to listen to at times, all make it an unpleasant sight to me. Slaveholders are very averse to selling their slaves at auction unless they are compelled to do so. Never have I seen more sad and sorrowful faces than I have seen at these sales. The sundering of family ties, the parting of friends are well calculated to make one unused to such scenes miserable. The everlasting cry of the auctioneer "& a going & a going $300. $300 is all I'm offered. She'll bring twice that in raising children in five years. Am I offered no more. 350, thank you. $350 and a going & a going, $350 and a going, going, gone." And then to see the burst of grief that she expresses as she may bid adieu to all she loves. And not unfrequently much of this grief is caused at sorrow at parting from her master who has treated her with kindness and consideration. As I said before, masters are averse to the slave trade and they heartily despise a dealer in human flesh.

Jan 27th Left St. Augustine today and after a tedious ride of four & a half hours arrived at Picolata 18 miles from that city. We had a very quiet time, no danger being apprehended from rapid driving, & the caution appended to the head of the way bill, "all running of horses strictly prohibited on this line," seemed to me quite a farce. Jog, jog along more like an old scow than a northern stage coach. We were not troubled by changes of horses and drivers by grog stations hotels or anything of the kind and very demurely walked up to the (what shall I call it) Hotel! no! tavern! no but to the frame or skeleton of the building where weary wayfarers wait impatiently for a boat to remove them from this dreary hole. A few moments after we arrived dinner (?) was announced, and our appetite as well as curiosity prompted us to inspect the fare. But oh! what a downfall to all our hopes when we came in sight of the table. A mass of smoky not smoking substances covered the table and one might very reasonably doubt whether they were intended for food or were in reality charred fuel from the fire place. We managed half sick to knaw at sundry bones and crusts of bread and wash them down with dirty brackish water and our only wish was that the arrival of the boat might save us from another & a similar infliction. During the afternoon our party was increased by another party from St. Augustine, Maj. Beard & wife & Mrs. Anderson. Supper followed & it fully answered all our expectations and was in substance & kind not unlike our dinner. 8—9—10 o'clock came & no boat, and now another question arose how we should spend the night. Mrs. A & B as a committee examined the beds and pronounced the safest course would be to camp on the floor. The night was severely cold and our room airy & cold. Maj. B & myself agreed to stand watch & watch to tend the fire, & we spread out cloaks, coats, shawls &c for our beds & retired not to sleep but to while away the long dreary night in listening to each other's groans, grumblings & complaints. It was a scene well worthy of a painter's pencil & would have made a capital charcoal sketch. Morning came & no boat & the day passed away in reading, dozing, and conjectures as to when the boat would arrive. Some thought she had blown up, others cast away &c &c. But evening came & with it an end to our misery for the boat came & we left Picolata. Of one thing I am certain, the inn keeper wisely concluded no man ever stopped at his house twice & so he made the most of his charge. From here we went to Pilatka, a place beautifully situated with some good houses entirely or almost deserted by the removal of the troops—and after another day we safely landed at St. Marys.[15] Pilatka now answers the description of Goldsmith's deserted village, for never have I seen a place of its size which gave such a sad specimen of loneliness and desolation as this. The large store houses & soldiers' quarters still show the expense which this Florida war was to our nation. Black Creek, the next place on our route, comes the nearest to total depravity of any village I have ever seen. The demoralizing effects of the war are exhibited in glaring colours by the dissipation, profanity & drunkenness of the place. I only stopped here for two or three hours and was happy to escape from a longer stay.

Feb 5th 1844 After spending a week very pleasantly at the quiet little town of St. Marys, I today have bade a final adieu to it on my way to my loved home. And I wish none a more sad farewell than I had at parting with some of my friends at this place. But I was right happy to leave my boarding house for even the accommodations of a steamboat. And as to the exchange of tables there is no comparison. They have a way at some houses of serving up ants with the dishes that is quite annoying to the uninitiated. And then such cooking. Tell it not in Gath, publish it not in the streets of Askelon. I even longed for the old dishes of poached eggs which we used to serve up in the counting room of a stormy winter's night. What a sad exchange for a pleasure seeker to make from the excellent table of Mrs. Reid to the poor miserable

[15]In 1853, when Mrs. Whipple had to go South on account of her health, Mr. Whipple was asked by Bishop Rutledge, whom he encountered at the General Convention then in session in New York, to help him that winter in East Florida, where he had no clergyman. Whipple held services in Picolata, Palatka, Jacksonville, Tallahassee, and other places. In his memoirs Bishop Whipple made no mention of his earlier sojourn in this region. *Lights and Shadows,* pp. 13–17.

quarters one is obliged to get at St. Marys. But 'tis over, and as all that is in the future is hoped for bliss, I will fain hope I may be freed from a similar infliction. Gen[l] D. L. Clinch and family and his bro in law McIntosh[16] were of the party and the passage to Savannah passed quickly away in pleasant converse. McIntosh has been a long resident of Texas and was for several years her minister to France. He excited our risibilities & our fears by relating some incidents of life in Texas, of Sam[l] Houston &c &c. The inland passage is a beautiful one as well as singular. It is a succession of inlets protected from the sea by a line of islands, and the tortuous channel, the forests on the island, the waving marsh grass that extending miles & miles looks like one vast prairie, all these have charms for a northern eye. At one time we are crossing a large bay, a small lake of itself, then we are hemmed in in a small passage not as wide as the Erie Canal, then we emerge from this to cross some sound in sight of the ocean and then again appear to be coasting along some beautiful river. With the exception of our sticking fast in the mud several times nothing happened to disturb the quiet & calmness of our passage.

We found only one place of any size on our route & this does not deserve the name of even a village. But it boasts as high a name as that of "a city." Brunswick was no doubt once a very flourishing city on paper and many men have cursed their stars that they ever heard its name. The good people of Boston were bled very freely in town lots in this city and the goodly city of Gotham does not make a nobler appearance (on paper) than does this same miserable Brunswick. A beautiful hotel was erected here in the days of bubble making and as hotels can't go without travelers the house is closed and gradually going to decay.

[16] George S. McIntosh was secretary of the Texan mission to Great Britain and France, 1837–39; acting *chargé d'affaires*, 1839–41; *chargé d'affaires*, 1841–42.

We reached Savannah today, February 6, in the midst of a severe rain storm and of course our prepossessions of its climate were far from favorable. I have met today our fellow passenger in the Lancashire, Mr. Heineman, and from him learned that the good ship Lancashire, Capt. Lyon & Mr. Eckford are without doubt lost.[17] It is of God's mercy that she was not cast away while we were on board on her outward passage here. But so it is, one is taken and another left and no sooner am I safe from danger than I am prone to forget God's mercies. Bade adieu today to Genl D. L. Clinch and family and Mr. McIntosh and only regretted that I was unable to enjoy their society longer. I have again met Mr. Sadler's interesting daughter, Miss Eliza Sadler, and was very happy to renew my acquaintance with her. I have also met Mr. Locke, editor of the Savannah Republican, an intelligent and sanguine Whig.

Savannah February 7, 1844 There is a large shipping business done in this place and much other business done for & with the interior towns of the state. There are many northerners located here who have been successfully engaged in business for many years. Indeed everywhere at the south you will find enterprising and energetic northerners located & successfully competing with those southerners educated & reared here. Such is the practical effect of the southern mode of rearing young men. In point of business talent I may say without danger of dispute that the preponderance is decidedly in the favor of the north. The society of Savannah is gay and to a certain extent very dissipated. The ladies are not as beautiful as I expected to find them and on the contrary there are more fine looking men than I have ever seen before in a place

[17] A quotation at the end of the entry: "A mistake, had a rough time & very dangerous but was saved."

of its size. Savannah can boast of some beautiful streets and some fine promenades. Its citizens may justly be proud of its beauty and of the good taste exhibited in the arrangement of the streets. Horseback riding is a very fashionable pastime and is much pleasanter than walking through the sand. I have visited the rice mills of this place and seen the process the rice passes through before it is fitted for market. First it passes through a set of mill stones, which bruise the hull & after this it is pounded by mortars until the kernel is entirely separated from the mill and then it is winnowed & casked. The machinery altho very simple indeed yet it is very interesting to a northerner to witness the process. The more I see of Savannah the more am I delighted with the order & arrangement of the streets & squares. It is certainly one of the best southern cities I have yet seen.

February 9. At 6 o'clock this morning we bade adieu to our comfortable hotel to test the travelling through the up country of Georgia. We took our passage for Macon on the central railroad—which like all southern stock pays the stockholders very miserably. The cars on this road are miserably constructed & the smoky stove bid fair to transfer us into bacon before we had half finished our journey. We passed through the counties of Chatham, Effingham, Bullock, Emanuel, Washington, Wilkenson, Twiggs, Bibb, which certainly gave us a miserable idea of Georgia land as it seemed as if we passed through one continual succession of swamps and pine barrens, as desolate a looking country as one could wish to see. An owl would hardly live here were it not for the mildness of a southern climate. I met a gentleman of the name of Varnum from the mining country of Georgia who made me a present of a sample of the gold ore found in the up country. The specimen he gave me was procured in Habersham County—and he seemed very sanguine in the prospect of realizing a fortune. We had nothing to interest us except watching the crackers at the stations & hearing their comments on the railroads &c. At one of the water stations where we stopped a few moments a nondescript of the cracker species was seated on a log by the side of some of our fellow passengers who were sunning themselves. The old cracker was smoking lustily. Says he to one of them "Stranger, I reckon my smoke ain't nohow agreeable." "No, it is not" said the other. "Well *move* then" was the polite reply. We reached Macon, Bibb County, at 6 o'clock P. M. 190 miles from Savannah & put up at the Washington Hall. Macon is a beautiful town situated on the Ochmulge River which with the Acone [Oconee] River forms the Altamaha River. It is a fine large town with a population of 6000 inhabitants. In 1822 there was but one house here. There is about 100,000 bales of cotton shipped from here every year. They have good schools here, a fine court house, market, and some beautiful private residences. The city is laid out with very broad streets (200 feet wide in many places) and is situated on rising ground, which renders it healthy except for a short time in the summer. The population of Macon is said to be moral & virtuous altho its business men are generally considered as shavers. They are linked in one with the other & all combine to buy the cotton of the countrymen at a reduced price if possible. But they sometimes overreach themselves. A cracker came into Macon a few days since & asked a high price for his cotton. The buyer offered him an advanced price thinking to pay him in depreciated bank paper—but after the bargain was made the cracker coolly told him he "couldn't take no money what hadn't got a buzzard on it." The business of Macon is light during the summer.

We left Macon at 8 o'clock and I may safely say on the worst railroad ever invented. Our northern corduroys are safe compared to this. The passengers are amused on this road by running off the track, sending rails up through the bottom of the cars and other amusements of the kind calculated to make one's hair stand on end. We only ran off the track once and that was in running backwards. I never have seen so wretched management. At one of the stations in Forsyth, a town of 500 inhabitants, we were detained 25 minutes for the men to chop wood for the engine. This is the first railroad I have ever seen where the cars were stopped to cut fuel. We were only seven & a half hours running from Macon to Barnsville, a distance of forty miles—at the enormous rate of five miles per hour. Bah! stage coaches can well laugh at such railroads. We here left this railroad, a pest to all travelers but a greater curse to the poor farmers who took stock in this wretched concern, for they are still worse off inasmuch as it has ruined many of them and now they are still bound for the debts of the road. We were unfortunate in suffering a short time but we ought not to complain while those who built the road are so much worse off. From here we took the stage coach for Columbus and it seemed as if we had jumped from the frying pan into the fire for we had a drunken Irish driver who persisted in driving us at the rate of 9 miles an hour and at the risk of our necks. Never have I suffered so much fear in the same time—every moment expecting to be dashed to pieces on the side of the road, but we reached Thomaston Upson Co. safe, & here I have stopped for the Sabbath and shall go on next week.

Stage proprietors ought not to hazard the lives of their

passengers with such brutes for drivers. There was one poor woman with her child in the coach who was the picture of despair as she clasped her child in her arms expecting every moment to be upset & perhaps killed. The planters in the up country of Georgia are more like our northern farmers. Their places are not as large as those of the low country planters. They have less hands and for the most part spend their life in the plantation. There are more of the peculiar southern phrases used in the up country than in the low country, more of the peculiar provincialisms that strike a stranger. There are many of these up country crackers who talk almost as bad a dialect as your genuine Cockney Yorkshireman. These crackers are singular specimens of mortality, real "lusus naturae." They have a high estimation of their own qualities & look on book larning as all superfluous. They are many of them stupid & ignorant & on the contrary you find some who are sharp witted & very intelligent. The people are very fanatical in religious matters & during public worship drive away all devotional feelings in a stranger's mind by their groans, screams &c &c.

I attended church today and heard some very good common sense sermons from three Methodist ministers. The church is in horrid bad order, for I counted 35 panes of glass out of the lower windows of the small church & I like to have frozen, for it is a very cold day. As bad as was the preaching yet I may say I believe it was good for me to have been there, for I had some solemn & interesting thoughts during the discourse. May God keep me from sinning against [*sic*] and guard me in the right path.

The staple of the up country is much less valuable than that of the low country, from $1/2$ to $1/3$ of its value, and altho for the most part small planters yet you will find some beautiful places and very wealthy planters. The negroes are worked harder here but are fed more, directly from the hand of the master. I have been much amused by the quaint looking teams that are used here in drawing cotton & other freight. From 2 to 6 & 8 mules are driven before heavy Dutch waggons[18] and the driver sits on one of the wheel mules, driving them as he would cattle by his voice & the crack of his whip. They camp out nights and nothing looks more wild & singular than the multitude of camp fires one passes in the night.

We left Thomaston Feb 12 at 1 o'clock A. M. in the mail-line which carries the New Orleans mail. This is an excellent stage route altho' the roads are wretched indeed. Each driver drives three or four teams and has no care of the horses. Nine months in the year they average 7 miles per hour including stops and three months 5 miles per hour. The land in this part of Georgia through Upson, Talbot, Harris & Muscogee counties is of a strong clayey soil & produces excellent crops. I was continually amused by the scenes around the camp fires of these waggoners and sometimes we witnessed specimens of the internal slave trade, as we passed the speculators with their droves of negroes. It is a money making business but one most men would dislike.[19] The clanking chain, the whip, the cruelty sometimes used have branded the traffic as one of horrid character. Far better for all would it be if our nation were free from this miserable trade. There are some instances of cruel separation, of terrible cruelties by some of these men, but no one here justifies them. As we neared the city of Columbus we passed some most beautiful

[18] A pencil insertion has been made here: "with corn husk collars & stick."
[19] The word "most" has been struck out and the expression "All having the feelings" substituted.

plantations; those of Maj. Baily, Seaburn, Jones Esq. & others near them are princely establishments & much good taste is exhibited in the arrangements of the grounds. We arrived at Columbus at 1 o'clock P. M. as weary mortals as ever travelled in a stage coach and at once took to our beds. The Oglethorpe house is wretchedly kept and is a lounging place for sportsmen, as gamblers are called in the parlance of the south. This is one of the most beautiful places I have ever seen, population about 4 or 5 thousand, and there are more beautiful residences in it than in any southern town I have yet visited. The streets are wide and airy and there is a very large cotton trade carried on here. The scenery on the river is enchanting and the beautiful Magnolia trees & pride of India add a richness unsurpassed to the scene. There is a great water power here which will be eventually devoted to manufacturing purposes. This city has improved much in morals in a few years but it is still a very wild place. Formerly street fights, duels, stabbings &c were served up at very frequent intervals and from the fact that it is a border town many wild characters have centered here so that in case of trouble they could immediately escape to Alabama. I visited the graveyard and Mr. Warner, a gentleman formerly of Oneida Co., pointed out to me the graves of many who had been killed in duels, street fights &c. Mr. Camp, a lawyer of that place, was considered a very bad one. He was shot down in the street. I had also pointed out to me the place where one man blew out his brains on the fence of the graveyard, where another shot his man &c &c. My poor weak nerves were quite unstrung while I was in a place that had been the scene of so much wickedness—and I must say I longed to flee from it. The law is still but feebly executed.

From here we left in the mail stage for Montgomery. The

land on our route is of a better quality than I have seen and
the planters appear very thriving. It is the ploughing season &
I am much amused by the most miserable ploughs used here,
mere apologies for ploughs. We met nothing of any interest
on our route except we had a little curiosity in looking at the
"dogries" on our route where the people were assembled
to drink. We had some amusing scenes on the way between
some of our passengers & the people at the changes. One
of our passengers was a genuine Alabamian and full of fun
& humour on the entire route. He was continually cracking
his jokes—but on asking one backswoodsman a rather boring
question he was answered in turn, "Did you ever see'd an owl,
stranger. What cussed big eyes they got, ain't they." We were
much entertained by descriptions of North Carolina given to
us by one of our number. N. Carolina is the butt of the south.
We dashed along rapidly on this route, as a cracker would
say, like a "whirl a gust of peck wood" or as nigger would
say, like a "locosmokus jinjim." The time was enlivened occasionally by walking up hills & by fording branches, creeks &c.
A part of our route we had six horses on acct of the horrid
roads. A gentleman who lives here pointed out to us on our
road the scene of the massacres during the Creek & Cherokee
war, and a great variety of anecdotes were told of Murrell's
gang, horse thieves, trunk stealers &c &c.[20] I forgot to mention
that at Columbus I saw one of the most beautiful courthouses
I have seen in Georgia and it is to be devoutly hoped that
with the new & elegant courthouse may come a new era in

[20] John A. Murrell, the "Western Land Pirate," headed a notorious gang of
bandits which operated in the lower Mississippi Valley. The gang, which was large
and fairly well organized, appears to have been engaged in almost every kind of
villainy, including horse and negro stealing, uttering counterfeit money, and rather
wholesale murder. Murrell was caught, tried, and committed to prison on some of
the lesser counts in the summer of 1835. The story of Murrell's exploits and downfall is related in *The History of Virgil A. Stewart, and His Adventures in Capturing*

Georgia laws. The land of Alabama is much better than I expected to find it, much richer than lands similarly situated in Georgia, and I think the planters are improving their lands rapidly. We passed some beautiful plantations, and saw planting life in the field. Negroes were ploughing & the overseer in the field with them overseeing the work on horseback. The slaves are worked here on the same plan as in the up country of Georgia. We reached Montgomery February 14th. It is a fine town of 3 or 4000 inhabitants and does a large business with the surrounding country. It is situated on the Alabama River in a valley surrounded by high hills on all sides but the river. The place is more moral than Columbus and its citizens appear energetic & active. I here saw 50 or 60 negroes exposed for sale & they were the best dressed & best looking negroes I have yet seen. They were apparently as listless and indifferent as could be and seemed to have none of that dread of being sold which negroes generally have. The buildings of Montgomery are generally indifferent altho there are some beautiful blocks. We passed through the counties of Russell, Macon, & Montgomery and Tuskege, one of the prettiest little towns in the country. The entire south dread & dislike Yankees and laugh not a little at their brogue as they call it—quite as much as do we northerners at those of the south.

Montgomery ships usually about 50, or 60,000 bales of cotton. Up to this time they have shipped about 28,000 bales and will ship about as much more. Here I first saw steamboating as carried on in the West. The busy bustling deck hands and

and Exposing the "Great Western Land Pirate" and His Gang, etc., compiled by H. R. Howard (New York, 1842). It is quite possible that Whipple may have read this little book or the preliminary account prepared by Stewart and issued in 1836. Stories of the Murrell gang crop up in numerous accounts of the times, and Mark Twain lifts one or two of the juicier bits for his Life on the Mississippi.

negroes engaged in loading cotton with their thousand provincialisms so full of wild boasting & bravado. The bluff at
Montgomery is 80 or 100 feet high at low water and the
cotton is rolled down the banks to the steamer. The rolling
of the cotton, the busy throng at & around the boat, the peculiar slang of the negroes, the wildness of the scenery, the noise
of the distant steamer coming up, all seemed strangely new
to me. I here first began to hear the "buster's" language of
the Mississippi. "Right smart chance cotton here, stranger!
heh!" says one, "going down the river?" "Well, I is hos."
"Look out there, (says the mate) or you'll run the thing
aground" &c &c. The different manner in which the currency
is reckoned in the different states seems singular to a
stranger as you pass from one state to another. In New York
we reckon by "shillings" & "six pences." In New England by
"nine pences" & "four pences." In Pennsylvania by "eleven
penny bits." In Georgia by "thrips" & "seven pences." In
Alabama by "dimes & half dimes." In Florida by "bits" &
half "bits" in Mississippi by "picayunes" &c &c. Alabama certainly is the most national in her currency for all small
moneys are reckoned by dimes & half dimes.[21] The entire
south & southwest as well as many parts of the north seems
very prolific in military titles for almost every third man seems

[21] This comment calls attention both to the survival of colonial nomenclature
and to the chaotic condition of the circulating medium as late as the eighteen
forties. The people of colonial days used the Spanish dollar as the metallic standard, the English standard for reckonings and calculations. The *real* ("rial," "ryal,"
or even "royal," when our colonial ancestors wrote up their books) or one-eighth
of the Spanish dollar was the measure of value, in metal, of the English units.
Hence nine pence in New England, a shilling in New York, eleven pence in
Pennsylvania, seven pence in Georgia, and a Florida bit all represented approxi-
mately twelve and one-half cents; the Mississippi or Louisiana picayune was equiva-
lent to a Georgia thrip or to a half bit.

When Whipple was writing, the silver dollar of Spain, Mexico, Peru, Bolivia,
Chile, and Central America, the French five-franc piece, as well as the gold coins of
Great Britain, Portugal, Brazil, Spain, Mexico, and Colombia were legal tender

to be blest with a military handle to his name. The steamboats on the western waters are very differently constructed from our northern boats. They are intended to carry large freights. The boat upon which we took passage had over 1200 bales of cotton on board & she is capable of carrying 2000 bales. The engines are on the lower deck & here the freight is carried. Above this is the cabin extending the whole length of the boat & above all the hurricane deck on which is the wheel house some 35 feet from the water. The Montgomery has a fine flued boiler & very powerful engines. The officers of the boat seem very polite & obliging—and the fare is low.

It seems strange to allow one's purse to rest as long as it can from Montgomery to Mobile for in this country it is proverbial that there is "no change out of a dollar," and a traveller may as well hold his purse in his hand ready to answer all calls on him. The scenery on the Alabama River is beautiful & in many places very wild & romantic. The river is lined for miles with high bluffs and is not unlike the Hudson R at the Highlands with the exception of the rocks which line its banks. Some of these bluffs are 200 feet high & it is an amusing sight to see the cotton come sliding down the steep banks. Owing to the many water courses & violent rains this river rises very rapidly & very high. During the last freshet, the river rose over forty feet and it would have done immense damage had it not been that all the towns are located upon these bluffs. The lands on the banks of the river are very

in the United States along with the gold eagle and the silver dollar. Government fractional currency was scarce down to the Civil War and was supplemented by the issue of banks and of other agencies which circulated paper and sometimes even metal tokens.

Alabama with her dimes and half dimes showed not only actual units of fractional currency designated and issued by the government, but a progressiveness in the use of terms. See Neil Carothers, *Fractional Money: A History of the Small Coins and Fractional Paper Currency of the United States* (New York, 1930), especially chapters 3, 7, and 8.

rich and of a loamy clayey soil. The bottom lands are generally covered with rich alluvial soil & nearly inexhaustible.
The planters' great staple for market is cotton & they are
generally wealthy. There is a large amount of shin plasters[22]
in circulation here & if a stranger is not careful his pockets
will be lined with this worthless trash. Small pieces of money
are here called "*chicken* money."

We passed Vernon, Benton, Selma, Cahawba (formerly the
capital of state), Portland, Lexington, Prairie Bluff, U. Peach
Tree, Claiborne & a number of other small landings on our
way down, none of them places of any note. Their business
is generally with the planters who ship their cotton at these
places. Alabama is a very rich state in lands. As we neared
Mobile we passed some large swamps and lost sight of the
high bluffs we had so much admired. I here saw the first
specimens of gaming which is so fashionable throughout the
western world. A game they call "poker" appeared to be the
game most played. It is said to be a very fascinating game &
one which none play well except old players. It is a game
which depends on calmness of mind & coolness of nerve. He
who can win & not be elated & lose & not be depressed will
make the best "brag" & "poker" player. Every evening we
were on board the gaming table had its votaries. Many
gamblers spend their time in travelling upon boats to catch
the unwary & obtain money. We had a very good table here,
and among other dishes I had a new one which is to the
Alabamians what hominey is to Georgians, "flannel cakes."
"Hulled corn" is a great dish here.

I was told a good story of an Alabamian's wit upon a
Mormon which Capt. Maryatt has incorporated in one of his

[22]Fractional paper currency issued by a bank or some other nongovernmental
organization.

works. "A stranger called at the Alabamian's house & was suddenly taken violently sick & soon died. A few hours afterwards two Mormon elders came along & avowed their ability to raise the dead, said they could heal all diseases &c &c. Says the Alabamian "Well, hos, could you do it if his head was chopped off." "Yes." "Well then," said he, bringing in his axe, "seeing you can we may as well be sartin & try ye" & raised his axe but the dead man bolted & since then in this section believers in Joe Smith's doctrines are few. I noticed in several places on the river masses of shells, oyster, scollop, conch & other shells 300 & 400 miles from the ocean. They appear to have been here ages & prove to me conclusively that at some time this has been covered with water. May not this be collateral proof of the flood & therefore of the truth of the Bible.

This route has been as pleasant as any part of my journey & I venture to say that to the stranger it will ever be amusing & pleasant. The great varieties of character, manners & habits one sees among his fellow passengers are a scene of constant notice—and had I been less anxious to hear from home, I should have enjoyed it. I saw some of the hardest specimens of our "free and enlightened" fellow citizens at the wooding places and landings I have ever seen. Men who never had an idea that did not savor of woodland life & hunting, real "genuine *busters*" "out & outers." Men who could out vie Dickens' Dick Swiveller in personal beauty and beat Davy Crockett all holler at backwoods talk. Such men are at least on the shady side of civilization if indeed they are at all troubled with that complaint. Besides these I saw some fever anatomies who were living personifications of Oliver Twist's poor face when he asked old Bumble for *more*.

Mobile is a town of about 15,000 inhabitants in the winter &

2,500 in summer situated on the Mobile River about 30 miles from the Gulf of Mexico. The land about Mobile is very low, and much of it is exceedingly swampy, which during the hot months renders the city very sickly. Much of the business part of the city is made land and during the rainy season the streets are nearly impassable on account of the mud. At such times the streets resemble miry stage roads more than the pavements of the city. This city was settled first by the Spaniards and has still quite a considerable trade with Havana & a large number of Spanish & French population. Ferdinand DeSoto visited this part of the south at or about the year 1540. In 1819 this was only a small town of 800 inhabitants & its business was very light, as but a small part of Alabama was settled. The business of Mobile is very extensive indeed—probably greater than of any town of its size in the United States. It is generally a wholesale jobbing business with the surrounding country—altho a large retail business is done here with the fashionables of the town. During the summer months the business nearly ceases and all who can, leave the city. The deaths for the year 1842 were as per the sexton's report 683. Last year the crop of cotton at this port during the season amounted to about 480 thousand bales but this year the crop will be lighter altho' it will bring a larger price. There are but few fine buildings in the city and it appears to be a place of business rather than of pleasure. Its streets are thronged at this season of the year. Some of the back streets are beautiful and out of the city in the piny woods are some beautiful residences of the aristocracy of the city. The morals of this place are bad, altho' great credit is due to the Alabamians for the passage of a law making it a penetentiary offence and $500 fine to carry concealed weapons in the streets, and this law has had an excellent effect altho it is broken daily. A theatre, a circus & several minor performances meet with a very good encouragement here. Gamblers and others of similar stamp and character infest this as well as many other southern cities, and meet with but little to intimidate them. A few nights since two gentlemen were robbed & knocked down in the street—and one of them his life is despaired of. The streets of Mobile appear to me worse than any I have ever seen. The transition from wet to dry is so sudden that one is either wading in mud or suffocating with dust. I visited today the planters' press for compressing cotton for shipping. The machinery is simple and yet so admirably calculated for the object that one steam engine working two presses is able to compress 1000 bales of cotton per day. It is done by means of heavy blocks of wood worked on screws. The lazy laughing singing negroes about the wharves make you laugh in spite of yourself. Such an array of flat noses and ivory you will seldom see—and then the merry sound of their voices as they sing "Ole Dan Tucker" "Yaller Girls" &c &c. There are a few of the tribe of Choctaws who still linger about their old hunting grounds & visit the city daily for selling of light wood. They are wretched & degraded looking objects, the miserable remnants of the nobility of the Indian race. The civilization of the white men has done but little for your people except to effect your ruin.

You can see as great varieties of character in the streets of Mobile as in any city of its size in the union. Clerks of all shapes and sizes; white & red haired men, staid thinking men, and brainless fops. Here goes a staid, demure faced priest & behind him is a dashy gambler. Here goes a quiet Quaker merchant and there is your Mississippi "buster," "half horse & half alligator with a touch of snapping turtle & a cross of lightning." Here is a walking tailor's advertisement and there is backwoods "Chickasaw hayman" all dressed "in yaller, pink & blue." Here is perambulating gin Cask, yclept a sot and yonder is an onion eyed Grahamite.[23] Here is a laughing nigger & there is a sad, sorrow smitten Indian. Here is a sailor just on shore with a pocket full of rocks ready for devilment of any kind and there is a beggar in rags. Pretty Creoles, pale faced sewing girls, painted vice, big headed & little headed men, tall anatomies & short Falstaffs, all are seen each full of himself & as if isolated from the world, so full do all seem of themselves. Oh! what an array of knowledge boxes, what a diversity in bread baskets, a great country this and no mistake.

I attended today a large sale of negroes at auction. The slaves sold had belonged to a very excellent master & as but few of them had ever been sold, they all appeared to be labouring under the greatest anxiety as to the future. There was one or two old negroes who were disposed to be quite witty. One of them expressed to one gentleman a wish to go back to Africa. Said the gentleman "this is a good country, plenty to eat, plenty to wear, make plenty of money here." "Eh! God makee money but no make it for nigger. Make it for white folks" was his reply. One old fellow said he did not care who bought him if they did not take him from his wife but "if they do, see if I work"—and the compressed lip told that he was determined. When the sale commenced, you could see the negro offered for sale show the greatest anxiety, his eye followed that of the auctioneer & as the bid came from a kind man his face would lighten up & his [eyes] brighten but when again the bid rested on some doubtful man his face would change, the smile would disappear, despair would almost rest on his countenance, & when he was

[23] Grahamite: a follower of Sylvester Graham (1794–1851), whose writings on dietetics persuaded many to become vegetarians.

struck down to the master he wanted, such a burst of joy as pealed forth from his lips I have never heard. These slaves appeared to feel a deep anxiety which was shown by the quivering lip, the convulsive twitching of the face, the suppressed tear, the heavy sigh, & the broken answer in reply to different interrogators. They all I believe had good masters. The auctioneer was a gentleman and used none of that low vulgarity which I have seen at some sales. And the citizens were free from all those low witticisms which some will use at such places. I was pleased to see a desire on the part of bidders to give the negro to those whom he would like as master. Slaveholders dislike to sell their negroes at auction as a general rule & will not do it unless obliged to—and buyers who want negroes to serve them prefer cheerful negroes & therefore they do not like to separate a negro from his family. But there is a class of speculators who care not how they sell negroes, provided they realize the most money. They feel no personal interest in the slaves, as do the masters & therefore to them they are only a commodity by which they can make money. But I have been pleased to notice at every sale I have attended here the auctioneer put up the family together & even if desired to by any refuse to separate them. There are, however, many cases of contrary kind. I have seen them where families were separated, where injustice was done, but we can only regret that such cruelty must exist, as long as there are bad men as well as good. There are many accursed instances of cruelty among slaveholders, there are also many noble instances of kindness & regard. These are the main, others are the exceptions. As long as this system lasts such cases must exist & they are the natural result of the slave system, as much & no more than are the cases of kindness & love. I dislike and ever shall the selling of slaves at auction.

I hate to see signs of "Slaves, Horses & other property at auction" because I never would wish that it could even possibly happen that family ties should be severed—and at all these sales there is danger of it.

The military of Mobile were out today the 22ond of February. It was a grand gala day with them and they made a fine show, the uniforms & equipage was in good taste & in good order & they drilled very well. Such independent companies are an honor to any place. The tone of society in Mobile is very gay and to a certain extent dissipated, altho' there are many here who prefer literature & its rational enjoyments to the theatre & gay revels. Many young men come here every winter in search of business and leaving behind them the restraints of home they become dissipated & rush madly to destruction.

The boarding houses in Mobile & its hotels except the Mansion House are far worse than those of Savannah. Indeed I have sat down at some hard meals since I left Savannah & were it not that the meals are harder where there is none, I should have gone hungry. Especially in the up country of Georgia I ate meals that would disgrace John Brown's track. Such a destitution of good beef and pretty women I have never seen as in Georgia up country. At the first boarding house I tried at Mobile I suffered. Roast pigs came on the table & such pigs. Could they have talked they would have said, "I am o'er young to take me from me mammy yet," and fish, oh! more like chips than fish. Oh! tell it not in Gath & publish it not, that I have eaten of such a bill of fare. I am now very comfortably located at Mrs. Jones and we have a good table and Mrs. Jones is an agreeable lady. I have been much amused at some of the countrymen dressed in red, green or blue homespun whom I daily see here. A gentleman told me a good story of his giving one of these fellows a Sedlitz powder. The cracker saw the gentleman drink a Sedlitz powder and supposing that it was some kind of liquor to make drunk come, said "I say, stranger, will you give me one of them blue & white things." "Oh! yes" said he & gave him one & went out. The cracker, not knowing how to drink it, mixed one in one tumbler & one in the other & first drank one & then the other. As soon as he felt it begin to work & effervesce he began to run about the room & holding on to his stomach, cried "I'm a dead hos & no mistake, he's pisoned me, he's pisoned me." The stranger had to explain & make apologies to save himself a flogging which the cracker's friends promised him.

They have a fine market here and I see daily all kinds of vegetables offered for sale, tomatoes not excepted, and I see by today's paper that strawberries have been seen here. Sunday morning is the great market day & then you may see all kinds of flesh, fish, and fowl, wild game, vegetables & fruits, eatables and drinkables of all sorts and descriptions—and then, too, all classes may be seen wending their way to the market. Black and white, rich and poor, all seem bent on making the Sabbath morning a day of toil, of merchandise, of money spending & money getting instead of a time for quiet reflection & meditation. The Sabbath is very indifferently kept here. Eating houses, groceries, apple stands & many other shops are open on this day, which shows that that solemn reverence for the day is not felt here which characterizes it at the north. This is to a great degree the case over most parts of the south, altho I have seen many places where the Sabbath is honored & cherished by all.

I attended church today at the 1st Presbyterian Church and

was much pleased with the sermon from Rev. W. T. Hamilton. Mr. H. is a powerful preacher altho he has an affected way with him which detracts from his eloquence. I believe his peculiar manners are natural to him, yet to me they are unpleasant. The text was "The people are too many that I shd give the Midianites into their hand lest they vaunt themselves and say our own hands have done this" and he made a beautiful application of the subject to the church.

I have felt quite sick today on account of the extreme heat and the suffocating air impregnated with dust. When the streets are dry, it is almost impossible for one to breathe or move. I never have been in a place where the atmosphere was as disagreeable.

Monday February 28th Henry Clay the great statesman & champion of Whig principles is in town today. He came on Sunday morning from New Orleans and was rec'd on the wharf by a large crowd of citizens, & a salute of one gun announced his arrival.[24] He is a very plain looking man & unassuming in his manners. It is amusing to see the crowd that watch his movements. "That's him, that's him" says one as they saw a gentlemanly man come off the boat. "No, I am not" said he, bowing. "There he goes" & away dashed the crowd to the other end of the boat. "Here he is, here he is, I see his face," said another & back the crowd came, pushing & jamming each other to see who should get the first sight of the lion. When Mr. Clay did indeed come along with his head bared it was amusing to hear the remarks made on every side "he's a horse" "he's a buster"—&c &c &c. At the south Mr. Clay is certainly a very popular man, but I have no doubt he

[24]Clay was conducting his preconvention campaign in behalf of his nomination for the presidency by the Whig party. The date (February 28) is obviously a mistake.

heartily is rejoiced when the bustle & noise is over & he can retire to a quiet place. I can fancy him passing through some of the up country villages in Georgia and it makes me laugh to think of the introductions that will take place as one having more brass than his fellows steps up & says "Mr. Clay, I believe." Mr. C will take off his hat & express his delight to see him while he heartily wishes this specimen of one of his feller citizens a thousand miles off. And then the work of introduction will commence. "Esqr A, this is Mr. Clay of whom you've heard." "Deacon B, this is Mr. Clay." "Mr. Clay, this is our minister" & then beckoning with hands "come up, come up, I'll introduce you." Oh! it's too good. The evils of greatness! The homage of the people is not always pleasant, if it is grateful to the feelings. Henry Clay is at present in the vigor of health, altho' passing into the sear & yellow leaf. He has a fine shaped head, one that a phrenologist would admire. When not speaking his features are calm & he looks like an ordinary man, but when engaged in conversation his face is animated, his eye glistens & the noble intellect is exhibited in every lineament of his face. He is an honor to America, & all Americans must feel proud of his talents, however they may differ with him in principles. He has great and noble powers of mind, a kind and generous heart. We may dislike the principles of action but we cannot but admire the mind & talent of the man. He is at present the pride of the Southwest, and adulation & flattery, as well as love & esteem follow him wherever he goes. The Whigs of Mobile are about giving him a ball estimated to cost $3000. Money poorly spent & worse than wasted, even if it is done to receive as great a man as Mr. Clay.

Monday February 26. Today I left the city of dust and business yclept Mobile for New Orleans by the way of Lake Pontchartrain. The distance is about 170 miles. The bay of Mobile, which you enter immediately after leaving the city, is one of the prettiest in the south. On either side you see the sandy beach with its range of woodland back, & the numberless small craft, lighters, schooners and sloops look like so many birds with their whitened wings. After a two hours ride you reach the shipping, which is unable to go up to the city on a/c of the shoal water, and it looks like an armada. I love to gaze on these evidences of national industry & wealth. Freights are very low as they are shipping cotton at 9/16. We had on board the steamer a party of North Carolinians "raal green ones," men "who had never travelled"—and perhaps "had worne all the hair off their breast climbing persimmon trees." It was rare sport to hear their remarks on the poles of the ship, the strings, ropes, bottom, top, shooting holes, &c &c. They could go to a woman's school a spell, as the Georgians say. The steamer "Day" is one of the best managed boats in the country & altho quite rough I enjoyed my trip well. In many places we were in shoal water & the constant heaving the lead, the hoarse cry ½ 3— ¼ less 3—½ twain &c &c rang in my head all night.[25] We reached the railroad depot at 4½ A. M. and after an hour and a half delay, took our seats for the city 5 miles distant. Much of the land on the line of the railroad is valueless on a/c of its swampy nature. Here we are at the depot and oh, what a collection of porters, cabmen & carmen, Irish, American & niggers. "Take your baggage massa," "want a cab," "a nice conveyance I've got for your honor" were about the kinds of salutations I recd. And after

---

[25] "3" meant three fathoms, "twain" was two fathoms, hence "½ 3" was three and a half fathoms or 21 feet; "½ twain" meant 15 feet. See Mark Twain's *Life on the Mississippi* (Boston, 1883), p. 106.

1. Mississippi River
2. Levee
3. St. Charles Hotel
4. Lake Pontchartrain
5. Fort Pike
6. Rigolets
7. Lake Borgne
8. Mississippi Sound
9. Ship Island
10. Chandeleur Islands
11. Gulf of Mexico
12. Proctorsville
13. Fort Dupré
14. Fort St. Philip
15. Fort Jackson
16. Balize
17. South Pass
18. South West Pass
19. McDonoughville
20. Algiers

New Orleans and vicinity, 1863

a ride of half an hour through all sorts of streets on all sorts of pavements I came to anchor at Mrs. Wooster, Cor. Canal & Carondelet St, Tuesday morning, 27 February, 1844.

Tuesday 27, February 1844 Today I visited the levee, and saw this mart of business. Such a motley crowd one seldom sees. The levee is about one mile long at its widest place & 200 yards wide. Here steamers, flat boats and vessels discharge their freight, and you see an innumerable quantity of barrels, hogsheads, cotton bags, pork hams, apples, bagging & rope &c &c. In fact this same levee is the market place of the wealth of the west. Nowhere in the U. S. is there such an amount of business going on as here. And then the speckled & streaked appearance of those engaged about it adds much to the scene. Drays innumerable in number are engaged in transporting merchandise to & from the levee and one is astonished at the immense numbers of these carts used. There are in the city over 4000 of them and these find steady and constant employ. This levee has been mostly made by soil washed up by the Mississippi which here has a powerful & rapid current the force of which is nearly 4 miles per hour. It is a beautiful sight to stand on the upper deck of a steamer and look around you and watch the movements of the busy bustling throng at your feet. Every variety of character can here be seen from the curious Yankee like myself to the busy restless speculator who makes this levee his world of action. Negroes of all shades from the Guinea black to the pale sickly looking quadroon, aristocratic niggers with gold chains & satin vests and working niggers, fat laughing niggers and thin sallow faced negroes who look as solemn as if they never smiled. Old men and young men, hoosiers, pukes, buckeyes, crackers, greenies, busters and other varieties of civilization are here

exhibited in all the eccentricities of their individual character.[26] Every variety of business appears to be carried on on and
about the levee. Steamers, schooners, flat boats & ships here
lie side by side & here the salt & fresh water tar meet. In one
part of the levee you may hear the cracked voice of some
bustling auctioneer and close by see a quiet sedate business
man who ever keeps on the calm & quiet side of business &
gets his fortune by patience & industry. Such varieties of that
peculiar species yclept loafers can nowhere else be found in
the south. What scant specimens of humanity; as you gaze
on them you wonder if it can be that these are immortal
beings and the noble beasts of burden around them perish-
able. Such half putrid masses of matter in their ragged tat-
tered dress, their rimless hats, their airy boots, their long
matted hair & unshaven beard. Can it be these beings ever
had a home, ever had mothers, brothers and sisters as others.
To see them lounging on cotton bales, whiskey barrels, enjoying the scorching rays of the sun, you would fancy not. They
have no ideas that do not savor of whiskey & laziness. No
employment, no friends, no home. Life is to them a dreamy
blank & death is to them the end of being. They have no fear
of undertakers, no dread of coffins, for to them these appur-
tenances of death are obsolete. The dissecting room or the
Mississippi is their grave. Every nation appears to be represented in this mart of business, from the hardy Scotch &
Swede of the north to the tawney Maltese of a warmer clime,
each jabbering away in his native tongue like so many mon-
keys. All grades of society, all classes here mingle & com-
mingle in all the peculiarity of their individual character; as a
western buster would say "stranger, if you want a tall walk
& want to see tall sights go for an hour on the levee." And

[26] See page 131, where Whipple explains these terms.

he who has not seen the New Orleans levee has not seen all of this great country.

Today I received a letter from home & in it heard that I am charged by some of my friends with being antiabolitionist, or in other words, a proslavery man. Now if to be opposed to the immediate emancipation of the slave is to be a proslavery man *I am one*. That despotism is theoretically wrong none can doubt. That it is right for men to be free none can doubt. But it is equally true that despotism is proper & best under some circumstances. The slave is at present unfitted for freedom, he is not prepared to exercise that noble prerogative. No! on the contrary his idleness, his ignorance, his lack of forethought & prudence make it preposterous for him to be freed. A Mr. McDonough near this place, a man of wealth, hit on a very good way to free his slaves. He called them together & told them it was his wish to free them but he also told them he was not able to free them, neither was it for their good. He first gave them a few hours of Saturday & promised to give them their time as soon as they earned it. In a few years they earned all of Saturday, then of Friday & so on until they had earned all of their freedom. These men in the time they laboured were the best, most prudent & careful slaves in the whole country. They went to Africa & are happy and contented. Now had Mr. D given these men their freedom at once, in all probability they would have become miserable thievish loafers, a curse to themselves & society, but by being obliged to learn prudence & economy & practicing it they became fitted to enjoy freedom. The theory of abolitionists embraces much truth but while they have preached that these things are all lawful they have forgotten that they were not all expedient. The bad influence of slavery in general is clearly seen by all intelligent men, but now the questions come up, shall we ruin the master & curse the slave by at once freeing all of the slave population. No! better to prepare them for freedom & then & not till then give them that precious boon which otherwise would be a curse.

March 1st The battle ground where Genl Jackson won his great victory is situated about 6 or 8 miles from the city & is at present occupied by plantations. It is visited much by strangers of curiosity & if you visit this place on a Sabbath, negroes will accost you & try to sell you bullets & other relics of the battle. Doubtless many of these relics are of a much later date than that of the battle & are only used as gulls or baits to procure money from the stranger. Among the mass of the citizens of New Orleans General Jackson is highly esteemed for his gallant heroism at this battle as well as for his other noble traits of character as seen in a long life, honorable to himself & useful to his country. An election has recently been decided here & it resulted in the election of Thomas Slidell, Dem. candidate to the Senate. I have met Mr. Slidell and am much pleased with him both as a gentleman & a man of talent.[27] The large foreign population of New Orleans gives to the elections a vacillating character and but little reliance can be placed on the result. Mr. Clay has many very warm friends here, chiefly among the merchants. He is very popular with this class of business men generally, chiefly on a/c of their prepossessions in favor of his course on the bank and tariff questions. I visited the house of legislature & will describe it after.

March 3rd 1844—Sunday. Sunday in New Orleans loses the quiet stillness which hallows the day in New England.

---

[27] Whipple must be referring to John Slidell, who was later Polk's envoy to Mexico and who figured, along with Mason, in the famous *Trent* affair during the Civil War.

Here it is a day of leisure not of rest. It is a day of toil, not in business, but in pleasure seeking. This is the day of *military parade* & review. Instead of being hallowed by songs of praise to a kind God it is a day of pomp & parade, a day when the music is dedicated to the God of war & not to the God of peace. I love as well as any the glitter & the show of a fine battalion. I love to hear the mellow bugle horn. I delight in the rat tat tat of the reveille, but oh! let me listen to these sounds on some other day than that which should be "holy." Then there is no charm in the waving plume & gilded dress, no music in the mellow bugle note & heavy drum. This is the day most fashionable for riding and all sorts of vehicles are brought in play. All kinds of horse flesh are in use from the dray scrub to the thorough bred racer. Gay dashing equipages with liveried coachman & postilion & humbler carriages are seen dashing along thoughtless and unthinking; they heed not the day. Balls & dancing parties are then given. Masquerades & dinner parties. Theatres & circuses are then open. Gambling houses, billiard rooms, ball alleys are used then as on other days. In the French part of the city stores are open, shops of all kinds, & the same money loving & business spirit is seen as on other days. Here this is a day of revelry & mirth, of feasting & dancing, of conviviality & pleasure—yes, this day of days, "this day that saw the Lord arise" is passed by as unheeded & unthought of by thousands as if there were no Sabbath. To such the rebuke of the prophet carries with force "Your new moons & Sabbaths are an abomination." Oh what a picture of moral desolation. What a depth of sin? Well might a philanthropist weep at such an exhibition. It was not until religion & the Sabbath were desecrated that the revolution in France assumed its appearance of terror & blood. Cock fighting, horse racing and other debasing amusements find votaries on this holy day. One reason of this is that there is a large mass of foreigners located here whose notions of religion are very vague & indefinite & either run into the scepticism of the French infidel school or the bigotry of the papists. The other portions of the population are generally business men & votaries of pleasure who feel not a sufficient interest in this city to try to stop the flood gates of sin & immorality. Besides there are many young men who come here & loosing the restraints of home & stifling conscience, rush madly to destruction. The military delight in parading in front of the churches and it is but a few Sabbaths since that the Rev. Mr Wheaton of the Epis. Church was obliged to quit preaching & dismiss his congregation on a/c of the noise & confusion of the military. Oh! what a wretched place to send young men to form their characters? Well may we blush with shame when such scenes are enacted in a Christian land. In a land of Bibles. In a land of sanctuary privileges. Little do the denizens of a quiet northern village know of the sin & wickedness committed on this day. Even while I write the rat tat tat of the distant drum is sounding in my ears & on the opposite corner is a crowd of people listening to the music of an organ player & a party of drunken Indians are dancing. No wonder they are debased & degraded among a people who thus desecrate God's day. But enough—I could write pages on this heart sickening subject & not tell the half of the wickedness of New Orleans in reference to the observations of the Sabbath.

The city is divided into municipalities, and the citizens of these different municipalities are as diverse in habits & character as the citizens of so many different countries. The first municipality is occupied by the French population and here the French language is mostly spoken. Stores here have

French signs, French clerks & French handbills. The streets are narrower & less beautiful than those of the 2ᵈ municipality and there is less neatness—altho there are some beautiful buildings, among which are the cathedral, the St. Louis Exchange, the mint &c &c. Here you notice signs in French and English & see all those varieties of character peculiar to French cities. Instead of "Phillippe St." you see "Rue de Philippe" &c &c. Gambling houses here have the names peculiar to such hells in Paris and all here looks foreign, looks unlike America. I was amused in passing through one of the business streets to hear the shrill sharp voice of a little dapper Frenchman who was acting as auctioneer in selling his wares. His mixture of French & English, his quite eccentric ways & his peculiar witticisms made me laugh. The morals of this part of the city are of that loose kind belonging to the Parisian school. The stores, shops and grogeries are most of them open on the Sabbath and as you walk through the streets you listen to the music of the ball room & hear the oaths of the gambling room & you feel that this is not home, where the day is honored. As I walked down through this part of the city today I saw two street fights, passed two balls, saw where there was a cock pit, saw several gambling houses filled with gamblers, in fact, all that could debase & degrade men seemed to be loved, honored & cherished here in this part of the city. It is painful to see the looks of those who surround these gambling tables. A few days since while walking on one of these streets with a friend, he proposed that we should enter & "see the crowd." Every grade of gambler might there be seen from the hardened player of fifty to the stripling who is just learning the catalogue of sin. Miserable shabby gamblers & jewelled gamblers. Men whose faces were lit up with a fiendish smile & those on whose brow was im-

printed in ineffaceable characters grim despair. Never shall I
forget my first & last visit to a gambling room. The anxiety
of some, the exhilaration of others, the despairing look that
told of ruined hopes—the bloodshot eye, the haggard features, the demoniac looks—all told me that if this was not
indeed hell, it was a depot on the way there.

The *Old Spanish Cathedral* fronting Parade Square is a
very antique building of the style of buildings in the 17th
century. This is the property concerning which there is a con-
tested law suit between the church & bishop. The house is in
bad repair & I believe its owners do not desire to repair it as
it would take from its ancient appearance. In the main body
of the building is the chapel & on either side are rooms devoted to the priests & the ceremonies of their religion. As I
stood in the deserted aisle & looked on its time worn walls, I
was filled with feelings of awe & I could not but think of the
past, & of the thousands who have here bowed to a gloomy
superstition & yielded obedience to papal bigots. There are
also some quaint old buildings in this part of the city whose
dilapidated walls and tile cov'd roofs speak to us of generations gone before us to the tomb. Everything we see tells us
in thunder tones or whispers in words of love "thou too art
passing away."

The *United States mint* is in this municipality. It being the
first mint I have ever visited, it was to me an object of
curiosity. The gold or silver is first refined to a suitable degree,
then run in ingots, then this is by machinery worked down
to the requisite thickness, by other machinery cut into the
right size, & then the impression given to it by the dies. The
machinery is simple & money is coined with great rapidity. I
saw them turning out the half dollars at the rate of 60 per

minute. The buildings & grounds are very good & kept in good order & the officers of the institution polite to strangers.

The market of this city is as great a curiosity as any part of it, not that the buildings are so beautiful or the produce for sale so fine, no! no! But the attraction is in the specimens of human kind exhibited there daily as buyers & sellers. All kinds of bipeds, fat & lean, tall & short, black & white & all shades & sizes intermediate. The songs of the niggers, the vociferations of the street sellers, the appeals of fat market women & pretty quadroons to buy, buy: your purse would be empty if as rich as Astor were you to answer half the calls on it. The stalls groan with vegetables of all descriptions. Green peas, strawberries, tomatoes, radishes, turnips, celery. Every kind of eatable that a tropical climate will give you & money buy is here temptingly spread out before you. Game of all kinds, venison, woodcock, pheasant, snipe, plover &c. Fish, flesh & fowl can be had in any quantity & you can see almost any kind of human specimens you may desire, & then the quizzing appeals, the merry laugh, the jovial song all make you animated & pleased. "Here, you tall man, buy of dis nigger" cries a fat jovial Guinea nigger. "Buy my flowers, Sir" says a pretty young girl who is offering you every variety of bouquets at only 1 bit each. "Taters"—&c &c is cried in your ears. Such a scene of confusion, of bustle, & noise would almost outvie the noises of Babel. Shrill voices & bass voices, modesty & coarseness. Beauty & deformity. Vice & virtue, honesty & crime come in strange contiguity at a market scene in New Orleans. The variety of languages, idioms & brogues, & mixed up with the provincialisms of our country, made it to me a rich scene, & amid all the celebrated razor strop man so renowned for his wit & humor crying "Strops, strops, a few fine strops left." This same hillman will make a fortune by this means if he continues to be prosperous. Such is a description of a half hour at a New Orleans market. This is the oldest part of the city, it was settled in 1717. Since that time it has risen to become one of the first commercial cities in the union. The second & third municipalities were but a few years since the suburbs of the city. The city is increasing rapidly and it is thought that all of the business of the city will be in the upper part of the 2ond municipality. There is but little change going on in the 1st & 3rd municipalities, from the fact perhaps that the foreign population of these parts of the city have not as much "Go ahead" in their disposition. As their fathers lived so do they, and quiet & contentment is preferred to bustle & business. In 1810 this city had but about 17,000 inhabitants and yet within a little more than 30 years it numbers nearly 200,000 souls. There was formerly but little shipping, now for four miles the levees & wharfs are lined with ships & boats of different kinds. This city must inevitably become an immense place and if unmolested, we can hardly imagine her size at the end of a half a century. Every year large numbers of buildings are going up, showing a rapid increase in population.

The second municipality is the abode of that noble class of humankind yclept Yankees, and here you see the development of that business spirit & enterprise as you can see it in no other place in the union. Business goes by steam, no time to stop and think, no! no! *"go ahead"* in its full force is felt by all and such an excited, restless set of men cannot be found in the world. Fortunes are made & lost here with almost the rapidity of the throw of dice. Such a dashing "go ahead" people are hard to be found and well may business be done rapidly for the work of a year is done here in a few months and then the city is nearly deserted by this class of business men, and of all the business done here none is so exciting as the cotton business. It is immense. Last year there were received here over one million of bales of cotton and this was bought up by capital here or shipped on a/c of owners to other ports for sale. A rise of ¾ cent has made men rich, a fall has ruined them. It is a perfect lottery, a game of brag where all the betting is done before the hands are shown. Every kind of deceit is used and it has been strongly hinted by some that even the United States mail has been delayed by bribery when important news has been rece^d from England. The responsibility resting upon agents buying cotton for others on orders is immense. For instance a friend of mine rec^d an order for 10,000 bales last season at a time when all seemed to forewarn them of a decline. He ran the risk and bought & from the change soon after saved for his employers in that purchase over 70,000 dolls. The capital used in this business is immense. Today only about 12,000 bales have changed hands and yet this small amount of cotton is worth 400,000 dolls. The number of vessels in this harbor at one time this season was estimated at equal to 2/3 of the entire shipping of the United States. There are now 273 ships, brigs, barks & schooners in this port and steamers in proportion. Yesterday the mail failed & I never have seen as much excitement evinced in trade in my life. Men might be seen in little knots at the corner of the streets and gravely (?) discussing the prospects of the market. This cotton business seems to me a perfect exemplification of the holy writ "It is naught, saith the buyer, & when he goeth away he boasteth."

This city is highly favored in her excellent fire department. March 4th today has been a grand gala day with the firemen, and they made a beautiful show. The dresses were in good taste & the decorations of the engines were neat & appropriate. One company "Jefferson" had a fine wild eagle fastened to the top of the engine & I have never seen a finer appearance than this king of birds made, as he gazed proudly around, as it were in sullen contempt of the efforts of man. The banners were rich, the paintings very fine & the inscriptions well selected. The juvenile members of the corps were not the least interesting, for they gave life to the show by their cheerful happy faces. All passed off quietly and it was a day which will long be remembered as a gala day of the New Orleans firemen. Such noble men who hazard limb & life in defence of others' property should be encouraged in those rational enjoyments within their means. In time of quiet we should cherish them. In hours of danger they will defend & protect us. The inspiriting music, the waving banners, the showy dresses & the trappings of engines & horses made it a celebration worthy of the city of New Orleans.

I visited today St. Patrick's church in this city. It is certainly one of the finest churches in America. The building is built of brick of the Gothic order of architecture and is to be a splendid place of worship when completed. The roof of the church is arched & the effect of the well arranged windows is beautiful, all the arrangements of the house are plain & rich & in decidedly good taste. Behind the altar are three beautiful paintings that deserve much praise, they are an honor to the artist who executed them. The characters of the figures are well studied & the expression is beautiful. The first is the "transfiguration" the 2ond "Christ walking on the water" & the 3rd "Christ healing the sick." We visited the church just at even, as the people began to assemble for vespers & I felt solemn to see the worshippers come in in that humble way & making the sign of the cross with the holy water, kneel down in the sanctuary. Altho' full of blind bigotry yet there is a beautiful lesson of faith to be learned even from the misguided Catholic. This church was built almost entirely by the middling classes, showing what zeal will do in the cause of religion. It is contemplated to expend about 15,000 more in finishing it.

The Catholic Church has a very large number of members in New Orleans, more than any other church, and I am sorry to say I believe her influence on public morals has been deleterious. The priests do not restrain the people from those fashionable sins which are so common in New Orleans. May the time soon come when this city shall be purged from her sins and be as renowned for religion & virtue as she has been for vice & immorality.

March 7, 1844 Today I visited the house of legislature and the Senate of Louisiana.[28] The state house is a dingy old building of quaint old architecture with bow windows & panelled doors entirely unworthy to be the capital of a state possessing even the wealth of Louisiana. It is situated on Canal St. and is in the midst of a very pretty yard of shrubbery. Having said thus much of the building, now for "the house." This body of the state representatives is much such an one as I should expect from a state like Louisiana. There are some fine talented men, men that would well represent any people in such a body, but the mass are somewhat sorry specimens of a people governing themselves. I saw some men who I am sure were never burdened with an extra stock of ideas & whose personal appearance was a little of the Dick Swiveller order. Dickens would have at once noted down the

---

[28] New Orleans was the capital of Louisiana until 1844, when Baton Rouge became the seat of government. In 1864 New Orleans was again made the capital and remained so until 1880, when again it was transferred to Baton Rouge.

amount of tobacco juice on the floor & the smell of smoke in the room. The intellectual character of the house is, I suppose, about on a par with that of Miss. or Penn. but not anything to compare with N. Y., Ohio or Virginia. The senate is a dignified body, containing men of talent and generally men fitted for the place. I was agreeably disappointed in listening to the speeches & remarks of members and I was on the whole gratified with my visit to this body of representatives. But I saw here many things I would have preferred to see otherwise.

In passing through the streets today I saw a novel mode of punishment, by standing in the pillory; the subject was a negro. His head was mounted with a fool's cap, a paper pinned to his breast—"Stolen $5.00." The position must be a very painful one, besides the mortification of being the gazing stock of a gaping crowd. I have also seen slaves at work as scavengers in the streets, male & female, chained to each other as punishment for some offence, I was told for criminal offences. An observing person who visits the south must of necessity see much connected with the system which is harsh and forbidding. He must see some cruel punishments & unkind treatment & on the contrary he sees much warm affection between the master and the slave. The evil of slavery is as great to the master as to the slave. My greatest objection to the system is the fact that the minds of this mass of laborers are entirely uncultivated & are left to ignorance & foolish superstition. This evil is great to the whites. The early opinions of children, their habits, are sometimes formed by slaves who act as their nurses. The religious culture of slaves is better attended to. They have churches of their own & are enabled to frequent the house of God & learn the truths of eternal life. As a people they are a decidedly religious people

& their ideas of religion are generally correct. And altho much of evil may be connected with the system yet the wholesale slanders of abolitionists are false, calculated to injure their neighbor & I cannot see how they can be prompted by a spirit that loves the neighbor as himself.

I visited today, the 8th March 1844, the Catholic burying grounds. There are three of them near to each other and they might with propriety be called "the city of the dead." Never have I visited a church yard where so many lay side by side as here. It would almost seem as if it was the design to see how many dead could be stowed in the smallest place. Here the dead are all interred in tombs built above the ground & during the hot weather the smell of the place is horrid. You wonder as you pass along if indeed it can be that these tombs do contain the dead, so many are there here. During the times when the fever rages the worst, it is almost impossible to procure for a friend a decent burial. Death reigns triumphant here at such scenes of visitation of the fever. Those you meet today are resting in the silent tomb tomorrow. A busy crowd of human beings lie in their last resting place, ere we had well missed them from our side. And yet amid these scenes of death, men become entirely reckless, laugh at death, forget God & many times are hurried from time into eternity ere the merry laugh had well died from their lips. They laugh & jest about these yearly visitations of death as if he were a welcome guest who brought in his train joy & gladness. It makes me sick at times to hear men joke about "Yellow Jack" & about old companions who as they say were in a hurry & went to breakfast in the graveyard. No! No! a thinking immortal being should look on death with solemnity and pious thought. He should not rush madly into the presence of his maker with the impious jeer on his lips.

The third municipality is in the north part of the city. It has less business, less population & less that is curious to the stranger. It is called the Spanish part of the city from the fact that there are a great many old Spanish families in this part of the city & some few old Spanish buildings. There are but very few Americans who reside here and it is improving very slow if at all. The city presents a singular appearance at night in the suburbs from the fact that the street lamps are suspended in the center of the street instead of being fixed in lamp posts. The better class of Spanish are excellent citizens, lovers of good order & morals, virtuous & civil to all; their only fault is in their extreme bigotry caused by an o'erweening attachment to a false & bigoted religion. The Catholics have a beautiful custom of decking the tombs of the dead, with garlands of flowers. It is a beautiful custom to thus pay reverence to the departed by daily visiting their tombs and wreathing them with flowers. It is a custom which is founded in our better nature, which softens the heart and mellows down the harshness & hardness of minds that have been chilled by constant contact with a cold & selfish world. Oh! how beautiful to think that when these frail bodies lie in the tomb, we will not be forgotten but loved friends will still hover around us & pay such sweet tribute of respect to our memory. Under such circumstances how beautiful & how grateful to the feelings is that beautiful salutation "May you die among your friends."

The morals of New Orleans! Start not, it may be a misnomer & perhaps I should have said the immorals of New Orleans. Whatever name you may apply to the subject, of it I will say they are decidedly bad & I would not desire a young friend of mine to form his character under the influences of this depraved city. I know other cities contain much vice, much loathsome immorality, & perhaps New York stands first in the catalogue of sin, but yet there this vice is concealed to a great extent. Here it is open, it is not concealed. The Sabbath is openly desecrated and that too in the worst manner by theatres, balls, circuses, cock fights &c. Gambling houses are tolerated, & these hells are many of them open on the Sabbath. Military parades are then held. None cry out against these sins and if they do they are unheeded. Every species of fashionable dissipation is acknowledged by the polite circles of the city. Drinking is an awful vice here. Oh! horrible indeed is it to daily meet these evidences of moral guilt & depravity of desecration of the Sabbath, of disregard of religion, of scepticism, of infidelity, of open vice. Money is the God worshipped and fashion & pleasure are followed by the giddy multitude with all the eagerness & delight that they would be if there were no hereafter. An apathy appears to exist in reference to most of these subjects over the whole community. Licentiousness, dissipation, disregard of religion & the Sabbath do not bar a man from an entrance into the best society. These same evils exist to a certain degree in all cities, but I think in none so daring in their effects & so openly seen as here in New Orleans.

I have noticed in all parts of the southwest a floating roving population, who are very loose in their notions of morality, who give themselves up to dissipation & profanity and who plainly show that Paley & Wayland, to say nothing of the Bible, are not with them popular authors and I fear with many Blackstone & Kent are entirely obsolete. I attended at Mobile a lecture on Shakespeare and his plays by a Mr. Hudson. Mr. H is a native of Vermont, a self educated man and one of the most interesting lecturers I have ever heard. He has a quaintness of style inimitable. His comparisons are novel, his figures and similes excellent. He gives you an excellent idea of the play in all its parts & explains to you the very ideas which you have had on reading the plays. He is chaste in his language and has a rich vein of humour peculiarly his own—eccentric at times in his comparisons, yet it is the promptings of nature & not the effort of a desire to assume a character.[29]

Negroes here in New Orleans have probably as great varieties in their character as in any portion of the south. There are as many shades of colour as there are varieties in character. An amusing scene took place at one of the hotels in the city a few days since between a nigger & a man who saw darkly on account of his libations to Bacchus. "Scip, you are a great man, you are Scipio. I can't hold a candle to you, Scipio, & you can to me. Now ain't you a great man, Scip?" "Well, among niggers I is some, but dis chile can't shine among white folks nohow." The nigger was the gentleman, the other a brute. The negroes on the levee are death on singing. The colloquies you continually hear are amusing beyond description. "Well, how is you, Cesar?" "I'se kinder fluctuated by dis spell ob wedder." "Is a mule like a jacaras, Sambo." "Well now he is, dat is a fac, only more so." These and similar colloquies may be heard daily on the levee and about the streets of the city. The negro is a bundle of oddities, of strange conceits and singular notions, and among them all not the least singular is his love of high flown words and his aping the manners of the whites. Some of the funniest beings I have ever seen are of the negro dandy species—so much gas & wind & smoke with a little charcoal is seldom seen. They are decidedly

[29] This paragraph is enclosed in parentheses.

bloods, as may be seen by the dashy dress & foppish air. Then there is your plantation nigger, of an entirely different species, coarser, poorer dressed and an entirely different dialect. He speaks a provincialism with as much of a brogue to it as cockney Yorkshiremen. He is too an oddity and sometimes possesses some wit & humor, which is most usually exhibited in his songs. Beside these are your real drunken loafer negroes, & working negroes, besides other species. They seem a happy race of beings & if you did not know it you would never imagine they were slaves. The loud merry laugh, the clear dancing eye, the cheerful face show that in this sad world of sin & sorrow they know but very few. There are some negroes & quadroons here who are very rich and many who hold property in slaves either directly or by proxy. Some of these free negroes make quite a show in their fine carriages and look quite like nabobs. But aside from their property & selfish powers of acquisition they have but little mind. To one unused to the confusion of a negro meeting such a scene would be quite a curiosity. Sometimes you would rejoice in your heart at their happy descriptions of their feelings & at other times be obliged to laugh at their foolish accounts of religious experience.

I have heard much of the beauty of the creole & quadroon population of this city, and altho' I too must praise features truly beautiful & admit that a black flashing eye & jet curls are beautiful yet I never see these quadroons but I pity them. I mean particularly those who are slaves.[30] To know that they are beautiful, to feel that they are admired & also to know that they are property & can not think & act for another must be painful & mortifying in the extreme. I never see any of

[30] The context shows that the writer made the not infrequent mistake of designating as "creole" some mixture of negro and white, apparently assuming that it meant some specific degree like "quadroon" or "octoroon."

these amalgamated specimens of mortality but I feel to pity them. I do not like to see such an amalgamation of colour. We have at our boarding house a boy as white as 9/10 of the boys at the north and yet this boy is & always will be a slave. He is the son of some white man & may have in his veins as good blood as any, yet altho white he must forever be a slave. I have not seen a place since I came south where there is such an endless variety of shades & colours as here, which speaks badly of the morals of some part of the population. As coolly as some may talk of amalgamation, I for one can never be reconciled to this heterogeneous mingling of colours. Give me either the blood of the white or that of the black, & for my eye there is more beauty in the thick lipped & flat nosed Guinea nigger than in the sickly, jaundice colored mulatto. Perhaps I might be able to appreciate the beauty of the quadroons had I my mind divested of the idea of amalgamation. But while I remember this I can not see any beauty in this compound of colours.

The ladies of the south generally are possessed of a different style of beauty from those of our colder clime. I think they are generally less beautiful. They have not that healthy rosy cheeked look which northerners generally admire. Their beauty is of a different order, arising doubtless in a great degree from the climate. They are well educated in all the minutiae of a fashionable education, generally accomplished, but too frequently the home education, as we term it, is neglected. Being educated for the south, where the servants are expected to perform all kinds of labour & where as a general thing they expect to marry wealthy, it is of but little consequence. But at the north, where most of our young men are obliged to depend entirely upon the efforts of their own, such an education is not of as much consequence as a practical home education. For a man of wealth & taste it may be a matter of very little consequence whether his wife is acquainted with all the minutiae of domestic life, but such an education is of all importance to a poor young man who must rise in the world solely by his own efforts. I have met many of the most estimable women at the south, women who I believe could & would adapt themselves to any circumstances. But as a general rule I am led to believe that for practical purposes the education of southern females is greatly deficient. The ladies of the south are well fitted generally to shine in fashionable life, they are educated for this, they expect to here find their sphere of action. But as I said before, a young man who has nothing in the world to depend on except his industry & energy had better select for himself a partner who is a "help meet" & not a "help eat." Long shall I remember some of my female acquaintances of the south, ladies who are unsurpassed in all those sterling attributes of character which make the female sex so lovely.

Perhaps on no subject of public morals is there so great an apathy as upon the sin of duelling. In the southwest especially duels are of very frequent occurrence. Seldom do you take up a paper here without finding some a/c of "an affair of honor" as these fashionable murders are termed. And altho duellists pretend to justify this custom yet I have never been able to see any justice in their argument. Had I injured the feelings of another, I know it would be a satisfaction to render him an apology. Had I been injured & slandered, it could not alter my character or prove the falsity of the accusation by my engaging in deadly combat with a fellow being. I would not if I were a duellist fight with any but a gentleman, & a true gentleman would never insult another who was a gentleman. I have conversed with many gentlemen who supported this practice & who had given & accepted challenges, and altho' they advanced many of their arguments on this subject, I have never seen one man who did not admit that duelling was in every way contrary to the Christian religion. It is contended that men show their courage fighting & not to fight is to be a coward. Many a man has fought a duel feeling & knowing it was wrong & only fought because he was too great a coward to say that it was wrong for him to fight. I think as great courage, nay greater, can be exhibited in refusing a challenge as in accepting it. Why it is that men look so coolly on this subject I cannot tell. Why it is Christians & moralists are silent is a mystery to me. Public opinion should be altered. Men should be made to feel that duelling was not only contrary to the laws of God but offensive to the feelings of their fellow men. Who could dare to carry through life the load of having caused the death of his fellow man? Who would dare to rush madly in the presence of his God from a duel? And yet men do do it, they shut their eyes to a hereafter. They forget the Bible, judgment & eternity and rush into another world with all their sins upon their head.

March 13th. For the last two weeks, the sporting world have been all interested in the races, which have just ended, and altho' I have perhaps as much curiosity as most men yet I had not enough to lead me to visit these scenes of fashionable amusement. Day after day have thousands visited the field & thousands of dollars have been lost & won on the field. Were horse racing confined only to the days of the week it were not so bad, but when the Sabbath is used for such purposes, then the voice of every lover of sound morality should be opposed to it. Indeed here this is the day when the races are most thronged, when men who have been immersed in business during the week go out to visit this scene of sport. I for one cannot see the beauty of racing at any time. What there can be amusing in seeing 3 or 4 noble horses under whip & spur & perhaps killing themselves with exertion I cannot tell. But when the Sabbath, "the day of sacred rest" is used for horse racing then none can doubt its immorality. Oh! when will men learn to look upon the Sabbath as they should, when will they feel that this day is holy & sacred & not a day for dissipation & gaiety.

The streets of New Orleans are very regular indeed, more so than any large city in the union. The streets are generally of good width and there are some fine public squares but none which can compare with those of our Atlantic cities. But they are very filthy and instead of wondering that the yellow fever visits the city, you wonder why it is not here all the year. Even now, before we have hardly begun to experience hot weather, the gutters are covered with a green filthy scum not unlike that of a frog pond & the vile odour which escapes from it is anything but pleasant to a man of delicate olfactory nerves. The streets back from the levee are lower than the surface of the river at high water, but instead of a steep embankment the slope is very gradual; indeed standing back from the levee during high water you can see the keels of steamers almost as plainly as if in a dry dock. In a climate like this it is of all importance that cleanliness be observed, and perhaps an ordinary degree of effort is used. But I am sure a stronger effort would be more effectual. But with all its faults I have never been in a city where all was quiet at night as here. Indeed it almost seems like a Sabbath eve, & you hear but little else except the watchman's rattle on the pavement. The police here is said to be very efficient indeed—and certainly the good order preserved is excellent testimony of their efficiency. For

I have never seen at any time the streets of New York as quiet as here.

The truth is New Orleans appears to me to be at the extreme of everything, the hottest, the dirtiest, the most sickly, and at times the most healthy, the busiest, and the most dull, the most wicked & the most orderly. They have in truth the most business, the best of land, the prettiest of women, the fastest of horses and the most delightful climate. It rains harder, it is more dusty. It is hotter and has a more diversified people than any city in the union. Changes take place here with almost the rapidity of thought. Today rich, tomorrow poor, today well, tomorrow dead, today hot, tomorrow cold, today dry, tomorrow wet, suffocating for air one day and the next suffering from extreme winds which almost vie with a hurricane in their fierceness. You can see here some of the richest & some of the poorest of humanity. They have here the first class of business talent as well as the "ne plus ultra" of loaferism. Dandies of the first water and backwoodsmen who care not for dress. Men of the highest intellect & fools of the first class. An observing man can see as much of the world & of diversified character here as in any city in the union. It is the grand reservoir of the great West. Millions of property yearly find their way here. And one steamer has hardly arrived before you hear in the distance the hoarse cough of another of these floating houses loaded with produce & teeming with busy restless mortals, and from one horn of the crescent to the other ships & other water craft lie in close contiguity.

A walk on the levee, no matter how often taken, is always the source of much amusement. It would seem that at each successive visit the scene changes, and you see new & richer varieties of character. The negro seems to sing more merrily.

Cathedral of St. Louis and Jackson Square, New Orleans, 1858

The laughs seem heartier, the hum & confusion seems greater. One steamer follows another so rapidly that there is no time to rest: each day is full of bustle & confusion. The varieties of pedlars, porters, carmen, carriage drivers, as well as the new specimens of woodland civilization mixed up with a few pretty tall specimens of "the everlasting Yankee nation" and haughty Johnny Bulls, make you laugh, if you have the blues never so bad. The amusing colloquies, the queer speeches & odd songs, the quizzing appeals, the jabbering of foreigners and the hum of voices, all now & then enlivened by a fight, "a gouging spree" or the like remind you of Babel.

Sunday 24 Mch 1844. Today heard a beautiful discourse from the Rev. Mr. Goodrich of the Episcopal Church. His subject was "carelessness of sinners." Mr. G is a man of fine talents & eminently fitted for usefulness in the world. I was sorry to see his small church so thinly filled while this city has so few places of worship and has a vast population. I do not believe 1/20 part of the population attend statedly a place of worship. To show my friends how the day is kept I will note down a few of the violations of the Sabbath & the scenes enacted today. 1st Three companies of military were out parading the streets and destroying the solemnity of the day by their music & show. 2ond Horse race of seven horses and this attracted many. 3rd A duel with small swords between a Mr. Richardson & Dubyes [?]. 4th A match fist fight for a $300 bet between two boxers. 5th A cock fight opposite the St. Louis. 6th Masquerade ball at the Orleans ball room. 7th Two theatres open. 8th French opera with ballet dancers. 9th Two circuses. 10th Exhibition of wax works &c. 11th German magician. 12th Organ grinders playing in the corners of the streets. 13th Stores, grog shops open. 14th Ten pin alleys, billiard rooms & other gambling amusements. 15th Several parties of pleasure to the Lake Carollton &c. 16th Italian Fantoccini. 17th Kentucky minstrels. 18th Ordinary ball. 19th Dinner parties. 20th Rides on horseback in carriages &c besides one or two lectures on subjects of such a nature as would be only made on a week day at the north. All of these I have seen advertised or seen today, 20 glaring violations of this holy day and each of which participated in by hundreds & thousands. Oh what a picture. If Paris exceeds it, it must be a hell and yet men say that this place is moral, that it is a fit place to rear youth & that he that says otherwise is squeamish, blue Presbyterian &c. If the Bible were not explicit on this subject yet for the sake of the well being of society the Sabbath sh'd be kept sacred and holy. One day in seven men sh'd rest & spend the time in reflection. It is to me alarming to see these glaring violations of the sacred & hallowed Sabbath & for the well being of this part of our country the lovers of religion & virtue shd make a strong effort on this subject. It must be done soon or the tide of sin & folly will sweep all before it.

And now, as my friends may have a little curiosity to know how I spend my time, I will give them an insight into the life of a genteel loafer, for he who does nothing is no better than a loafer. As the mornings are too damp to go out and are considered unhealthy it is a good excuse to lay late in the arms of old Morpheus & 7 o'clock is the earliest hour of rising. A little time spent in reading & then breakfast, then a walk to the post office and an hour or two perusing the sage remarks of the editors of the papers. A little chit chat & then a half hour's crowding & jamming to get to the box for delivery of letters. Then a half hour of reading letters, or in thinking of the probable reasons of not receiving letters. Each mile of the long route is travelled over in imagination and thousands of vain conjectures are indulged in. A stroll to the auction rooms, a walk on the levee or a visit to some friend finishes the morning & then comes dinner. After dinner letter writing, writing in my journal or a touch at Spanish finishes the day, and the evening is spent in reading, gossip or listening to the sweet music discoursed to us by the Italian harpers who come here nearly every evening to play for the crowd. And thus one day passes with another. This is the first winter I have ever tried the sweets of continual idleness & I fancy will be the last, for all miseries deliver me from the ennui of being idle. For man to enjoy this fleeting world his mind & body needs constant employ. Idleness & inactivity are the worst of miseries for a human being to endure. No matter by what pleasant euphonious name it may be called, idleness is the same, a life of misery. But adieu to this essay on loafing. I expect tomorrow to take up my line of march for the north and at least there is one consolation, that I shall have a new scene for my business even if the business should not be changed, and so adieu to my journal until I leave this great city, great in business, in gaiety and also in vice & dissipation.

Today, March 30th, having packed up bag and baggage, paid all bills and made all calls I am off up the Mississippi. The Missouri on which I have secured a passage is one of the finest boats on the river. She has two engines of 600 horse power, each a wheel 33 feet in diameter, and is 280 feet long by 40 feet wide. Her cabins are spacious and airy and her state rooms are as neat and commodious as any I have ever seen, being about 8 feet square. The fare is only $15 to St. Louis, a distance of 1100 miles, and you are boarded. But enough of the boat. And now comes the most unpleasant part of human life, the parting. I always dread to hear that sound "Farewell" whether it may be spoken by an old and much loved friend or spoken in kindness by one whom I have known but yesterday. I bade them all adieu, friends, acquaintances & relatives, & leave with them all my heartiest & kindest wishes for their future welfare. Here I am on the boat, the last farewell has been given and again, as I have often been, I am a stranger among strangers in a strange land. The scene at the levee at the time boats leave is very interesting to anyone who is like myself "a looker on in Venice." You are besieged until the last moment by newspaper sellers, by book pedlars, candy women, fruiterers & others who are as importunate as possible to buy! buy! And then such a crowd of friends parting, acquaintances bidding adieu and the bustle of porters, carmen, shippers, clerks running with bills of lading to be signed and others with packages of letters to be mailed. The noisy swearing deck hands and the commanding voice of the Capt. all seem to make confusion worse confounded. "All ashore" is cried & away scatter the crowd while the heavy steamboat bell tolls for you all an adieu. Whiz, puff, puff and back we go into the stream, a revolution or two of the wheel and at the signal the cannon is fired and away our noble boat rushes on her course like a steed under whip & spur. The last glimpse of the noble crescent city has just faded in the distance and here we are on the dark turbid water of the mighty Mississippi. The weather for the last few days has been excessively sultry and so hot I have suffered severely, while today the 30th March it was so cold a few scattering flakes of snow have fallen. Such changes as this are very unusual anywhere. Blackberries had appeared in market as well as other fruits & vegetables which we do not get in Jefferson County until July.

The scenery for many miles is delightful. The rich plantations, with their beautiful houses & neat cabins for the negroes, with the green foliage which nature has already arrayed herself in, form a scene to me peculiarly beautiful. These lands are lower than the Mississippi is at present and are only protected from overflow by the levee, which is an artificial embankment thrown up 12 to 20 feet wide & of a sufficient height to protect the land. The river is here as well as in most parts of it very crooked and winding and the ever changing scene as you round a point is pleasant altho' I suppose in a few days I, like all others, will feel wearied by it. The deck hands of a Mississippi steamer are as hard apologies for human beings as I ever saw. They glory in a "row," a "fight" or "spree" and I know of no charm about this class of men except their fine singing when leaving or coming into port. Then they use their voices to good purpose & it is pleasant to hear them. But adieu, my note book, until tomorrow.

There is probably no route in the union where a stranger sees a greater variety of character and more diversified scenes than on this mighty river, the "father of waters" as it is rightly called. Its great length and the large body of water which thus finds its way to the ocean are enough to give it a great name, but it is of far greater importance when we remember that it bears on its bosom the wealth of the west, carrying to its market millions of dollars worth of valuable products and returning to these states again the produce of other & distant portions of the globe. The current is powerful and in many places very rapid. Large flat boats looking like huge hog pens & yclept "arks" may be seen in great quantities here which are only used to descend the river, and the merry song or coarse laugh of these "busters" sounds singularly enough as you pass them on their way to New Orleans. At the mercy of every eddy and whirled here & there by the current, yet they safely reach their haven. What an isolated life to be shut up weeks in one of these floating pens, no excitement, no business, nothing to do but doze in the sun or watch with idle curiosity their course as whirled here & there by the strong current. Now & then by way of amusement they stop at some of the landings and "kick up a fight" just by way of showing the natives what a " 'arf 'orse & 'arf allegator" can do. All kinds of western produce is thus brought to market at a very cheap rate. Only think, there are now on the Mississippi & its tributaries about 450 steamboats and in 1811 the first steamer was built at Pittsburgh. You have hardly passed one of these floating palaces and heard the last echoes of its blowpipe ere you hear ahead another coughing as if in the last stages of consumption, each freighted with goods & produce & teeming with human beings. Here & there the Captain will gently excite your nerves by pointing out the spot where a steamer was lost, by snagging, bursting or running aground or afoul of another boat. Of one thing all are convinced, that travelling here is far from being free from many dangers.

No one unacquainted can imagine the extremely winding course the river has. You will many times pass bends where the channel runs 20 to 30 miles around a bend when it is hardly a mile across. The channel is continually changing and one man loses large parcels of soil which go to enrich his neighbor and thus trees & large bodies of land are washed away by the mighty volume of water and many times these trees become embedded in the mud and form snags or "Mississippi sawyers." The current is very powerful and rapid, which greatly impedes navigation. In many places it is 4 miles per hour & even more. The width of the river is very unequal, but generally from a ½ mile to a mile & a half wide. The lands you see on either side are generally rich and fertile and in many places the scenery is very picturesque & beautiful. The quiet plantation, the neat white houses, the fertile lands, the green crops and the busy negroes form a very pretty view. Here and there in some lonely parts of the river, the tall trees with their drooping limbs covered with hanging moss look gloomy and almost make you sad. It is from 20 to 100 feet deep and the navigation need only be dangerous from the prevalence of "sawyers," which are gradually disappearing before Uncle Sam's snagboats. The civilization of most of the people here is "mighty wild in its nathur" as the Irishman said and might too frequently is right. Gambling is a common mode of amusement on the river and so great is the passion for it that men have lost in a night their all, and bereft of property and character been left to dark despair. A gentleman told me a story of a Frenchman to illustrate the power of it. His wife was with him, in the ladies' cabin, sick, and he was told of it. He gambled on. Again told she was worse—but still fascinated he played on. At last he was told she was dead. "Ah!" said he, "no use. 10 dollars better. Me no help it." Brig[31] & poker are the great games played and many is the man that has been poked out of character, money & all by this worst of gambling games. Each evening finds the gambling table & its votaries employed & not to gamble is considered by these natives as to be rather squeamish. Altho' the moral & better portion of community are setting their faces against it & in Louisville they have formed a "Reformed Gamblers" society.

The river overflows its banks in many places during the times when it rises. It rises in some places and at some times from 25 to 50 feet. Being the great drain for the west & having so many tributaries, one would suppose its spring freshets

[31] "Brig" may mean "brag," a game similar to and derived from draw poker. *American Hoyle* (New York, 1864), p. 169.

would sweep all before it. In some places the river overflows its bank 10 miles back. In the lower part of the river the lands are protected from these overflows by raised embankments called "levees" altho' the protection thus afforded is far from being a certain one. The timber on the banks is very diversified in character, but on most parts of the river cotton wood is the *"staple."* I ought here to mention that I have as yet seen no gambling on our boat and think our passengers are very moral. The towns between Natchez and New Orleans are small and of no importance. Donaldsonville was once of some note as it was formerly the capital of Louisiana.[32] Biou Lara, Fort Adams & the other small towns are of no note and the time spent in visiting them would be labour lost. As we passed Fort Adams the high bluff on the river near there made me think of home and I was much amused by the joyful exclamations of a German "Dat is very goot, verry much make me tink of mine country."

Natchez is a place of about 5000 inhabitants 292 miles from New Orleans by the course of the river and 155 miles by land. Natchez under the hill is a vile place filled with boatmen and low characters and was once as renowned for vice as the fine points. Natchez above the hill, the city proper, is a beautiful place situated on a high bluff and laid out in an oblong form. The ground is quite uneven and altho' the streets are very regular indeed yet it detracts from the order & regularity. The houses are very neat in their appearance and many of them have pretty porticos in front and neat gardens around them. The place has done and is still doing a good business, chiefly in the cotton trade, for which staple this is a great market. Ships sometimes ascend as far as here for freight. The great width of the streets and the airiness of the situation

[32] One wonders how Whipple got this bit of misinformation.

ought to make it healthy. In morals it is of the same school as other southwestern towns and I suppose many things are winked at here which would not be tolerated in the north.

We reached this place in 25 hours & a few minutes. The time has been made in 22 & a few minutes but we were delayed by mending machinery and by a monstrous wind. The numerous flat boats and rafts & the passing steamers have thus far amused me. I could not have imagined that the river was so extremely crooked. The small towns on the river between Natchez and Vicksburg are destitute of interest & seem to be as dull as the wooding places on the river. These wood yards are on the banks of the river and they put wood on one of these boats with a rush at the rate of 30 or 35 cords per hour. This boat uses about 500 cords on a trip up and down and this costs about $1000, being about 1/3 of the whole expenses of a trip. She can hardly make 2 trips in a month. So if one of these boats are not making they are losing money very fast—$3200 were the expenses of the last trip. Last trip she brought down on herself and the barge she towed over 1700 tons of freight & she had $1000 for towing down the barge.

Vicksburg is a beautiful place and situated on a side hill. The houses are in clusters scattered here and there over the declivity. The streets are of good width and the people have considerable enterprise. It is not many years since it was set-tled and is a new town. It has good land about it & as usual cotton is the "sine qua non." The harbour is good here, & you will generally see steamers lying here. It was here that the people, outraged by the character which these travelling blacklegs had given their place & feeling that the law was ineffectual to put a stop to it, resorted to the old first principle "might is right," and by a decision of Judge Lynch's court hanged them on a tree. I had the locality of the tree pointed out to me. It is situated on the back part of the town near the burying yard. Long will Vicksburg be designated as the place where the gamblers were hung without judge or jury. The place does a very considerable trade and appears well, population about 4000 & located on the east side of River about 400 miles from New Orleans. I was greatly amused here by the parting of 2 Irishmen from their cronies as they came on board bound for upper Mississippi. "Patrick and if indade and we don't see each other again in this grate counthry, you'll never forget the boys who lived with you in swate old Ireland." "And so God bless ye & kape ye whin away in the wild country." Honest hearts! Your kind farewell made even me rejoice in Pat's happiness. The citizens may have acted very unwisely in giving such an example of mob law but all agree that the provocation was very great. They had long had this band of desperados, gamblers, blacklegs & rascals prowling among them beyond the reach of all law and destroying all that renders a place dear to any people. The people met, determined to put it down, not intending to injure anyone but only to destroy the house which was their rendezvous and make them leave. As they came to the house and burst open the door, a D. Bartton was shot, a man who was much loved & esteemed by the people. They seized four of the leaders & the man who kept the house, & with ropes around their necks executed summary justice upon them and gave notice that all other gamblers would be treated in like manner unless they left the town in 10 hours, and now when these roving sporting characters assemble here it is only necessary for the paper to warn them that a "certain tree" is still standing to cause them to leave.

This whole section of country was once inhabited by a band

View of Vicksburg, Mississippi, 1855

of villians who lived by plunder & rapine. Above here in the borders of Arkansas was the place where the famous Murrell gang met to concoct their diabolical schemes, but these scenes are disappearing and men can now travel through this country in comparative safety. Near Lake Providence some 35 years since there was a band of robbers who were wont to entice boats ashore & live by plunder & murder. The light of religion & virtue is still needed to scatter away the last traces of this bloody spirit. But the settlers who are now here are trying by all means in their power to make this rich and fertile country a land of peace & quietness, where once the land was governed by fear & violence. Duelling and other acts of similar nature are of far less frequent occurrence than formerly & I hope the time is near when all such scenes shall be banished from our land.

Last night we were all alarmed by the cry of fire, and there was a general rush to see what & where. Some screamed, others were for having the boat landed &c &c. It proved to be a barrel of clothes sitting back of the ladies' cabin which had taken fire from a spark—and after this was thrown overboard quiet was restored. I have never been on any boat where I was more pleased with officers, crew & boat and she is a very fast boat, one of the fastest on this river. We have had some delays and we reached Memphis in 2 22^{½} 24^{33} a distance of over 800 miles from New Orleans.

Memphis is a place of considerable importance situated on an elevated bluff and scattered over a large space. It has a large trade with the surrounding country and ships a great deal of cotton, about 80,000 bales. This cotton is not as good as that raised farther south. This city has a population of over 4000 and is a thriving place. A railroad terminates here from

[33] One guess is as good as another as to what the writer meant by these figures.

the interior and the land around here is of the best quality.[34]
In morals I should judge, from the physiognomy, that it re-
sembled our northern towns more than New Orleans, altho
from being a border town and situated on the river it will
always be more or less filled with bad & immoral characters.
The towns between here & Vicksburg make a better appearance on paper than in reality & were destitute of all interest
except as I here and there saw some swarthy backwoodsman
who could claim the title of a genuine buster. I saw many
such at different points on the river & I am inclined to think
a small "spec" could be made in taking them north to exhibit.
When I reached "Napoleon" I could almost imagine I had
reached Onondaga County and was again there among the
paltry villages which have taken to themselves the names of
the mighty dead. Here as well as elsewhere in Arkansas I
saw some tall specimens of "hosses" and gals too. One of
which were I a painter I would paint in all her glory dressed
"a la mode," only more so, and the way the baser metals were
used up on her was "curous." I reckon she could ask a man
with all ease in the world "Well, hos, let's take a trot" that is
to say, dance a jig. Henry Clay was travelling through this
country and attended one of these back woods "flareups"
and of course had to play the agreeable to the fair sex, so said
he to one of the girls "Will you dance." "Well, I will, horse,"
putting the statesman almost to blush.

Wednesday April 3, 1844. Well, here we are at "Cairo"
not the far famed Egyptian city whose renowned name has
spread throughout the globe but a quiet "paper" city at the
junction of the Ohio with the Missisippi. It is a scant pattern

[34] It must have been that Whipple heard about a railroad which had been chartered but not built, for no railroad was in operation in western Tennessee at this
time.

of a city, scant in houses, scant in property, scant in business, scant in population, but Oh! it's great on paper. We have made the trip from New Orleans to this place in 3 days and 19 hours, a distance of 1000 miles. No wonder these splendid steamers bear the name of "Mississippi race horses." Every day that passes, I wonder at the number of these "coughing monsters." Their name is legion. Of all places to see "natur" as Sam Slick calls it, go to New Orleans and then up the Mississippi. You can see the "buckeye" of Ohio. "The puke" of Missouri. "The sucker" of Illinois. "The Hoosier" of Indiana. "The wolverine" of Michigan. "The horse" of Kentucky. "The mudheads" of Tennessee. "The busters" of Mississippi. "The 'arf hoss & 'arf alligator" of Arkansas & many other specimens, as "corn crackers," "crackers," "Chickasaw hay men" & "*live* Yankees" in all the richness of their character. One & all have chosen one motto "Go ahead" and they do it too.

About 30 miles from Cairo is a place called "the Graves" where a great many steamers have been lost by snagging and a melancholy place it is too. Dreadful is it to think that such numbers of human lives are yearly lost by the carelessness of the officers of the boat. I have heard that in all nearly 500 lives are lost annually on these waters. I find my good opinion of the excellent morals of our passengers was doomed to a downfall as they now gamble all the time (that is some of them), but of one thing I am satisfied, the Sabbath was not broken.

The other towns on the river above Cairo, St. Genevieve, Cape Girardeau & Kaskaskia are of no note; those named are very old, having been settled for trading posts. At Cape Girardeau the Catholics have recently erected a fine brick edifice to be used as a university. In all of these old French settlements the Catholics are numerous. The scenery above the mouth of the Ohio is of a different character & on either side you see lofty rocky bluffs and more gentle hills and the scenery is more of that wild and beautiful character, which is so characteristic of the Hudson River. The navigation is more dangerous & we passed several boats that had been sunk within a few days. But I see by the merry singing of the crew we are at St. Louis, having made the trip in 4 days, 12 hours.

The rough cragged hills which I here saw reminded me forcibly that I was again returning to my home in the north. The change of lowland scenery for that hilly, wild & romantic landscape view which I here saw in all its beauty was an agreeable one. Men may prate forever of the beauty of southern views and southern scenery, and altho' I admire it as well as others, yet for me there is far more beauty in the ever changing scenery found in more northern latitudes. The scenery on the river above the mouth is of the most beautiful character, especially near the "Devils Rocks" and by Cape Girardeau and Kaskaskia. At each turn in the river you meet newer and wilder scenery and you would fain linger there to gaze on the diversified scene around you. There is some very fine table land near St. Louis on the Illinois side and these level lands surrounded by higher land look very beautiful. The prairie country is beautiful and none can delight more than I in the fertility of these western states. When their resources are fully developed then will this be the garden of the New World. This section of country as well as the more southern states is full of provincialisms and you are constantly hearing phrases of which you know not the meaning—such as—"That's *corn*" meaning "That's first rate." "Run the thing aground" meaning "He will overdo the matter." "Biler

Cathedral. P.Church. E.Church. Court House. B Church. B Hotl.

Hall Tobacco Ware House. St Louis University

View of St. Louis

(from a print found in the original diary)

is bust" meaning "He is broke down." "A pocket full of rocks" meaning "a large sum of money." "He is a hoss" meaning "He is a smart man." "It's mud & no mistake" meaning "rich land without doubt." "Mighty curous" meaning "very singular."

If Dickens, Mrs. Trollope & other English writers find fault with the curiosity of Yankees, and all admit they are a little inquisitive sometimes, what would they not say of the curiosity of some of these Western backwoodsmen. Not only do they desire to know all, but for fear you may have not told all they will be sure and ask you many a question of matters and things of no consequence to them & of which they are as well acquainted as you are. As a specimen of the coolness of some of these quizzers, as I walked up into the city today faster than the drayman, I had to ask the way to the Planters Hotel & inquired of a man standing in the street. "Stranger eh!" said he, eyeing me. "Where may you be from?" After answering him and telling him a few items of news, he told me where the hotel was. This is only one instance of this peculiar habit of inquiring into others' business.

I believe I have seen more "natur" since I left home than in all my lifetime before. I am quite sure I have seen some specimens of mankind entirely new and strange & of whose existence I was before entirely unacquainted. And among them all there is a greater recklessness of human life than east. As a Mississippi fireman said "Talk about northern steamers, it don't need any spunk to navigate them waters. You haint bust a biler for five years. But I tell you, stranger, it takes a man to ride one of these half alligator boats, head on a snag, high pressure, valve sodered down, 600 souls on board & all in danger of going to the devil."

St. Louis is a very fine city situated on the west bank of the

Mississippi and is of great commercial advantages, being the outlet of all the products of these rich north western states & territories. It has been and is continually improving and is destined to be one of the first cities in the union. It was settled in 1764 in February by Mons. Laclede & others and named after Louis 15 the King of France. It was settled for a trading post and from its locality had then great advantages. Soon after its settlement it was made a military post, and was the capital of Upper Louisiana. In 1768 it went into the hands of Spain and remained in their hands until 1800 when it again went into the hands of France & was sold to us in 1804. The fur trade soon after induced many English settlers to settle here and since then it has become a great and powerful city. It is situated on a high bank and is very well located. It is a continued & gradual ascent from the river, the streets running to the river brink. In 1817 the first steamer came here and in 1822 it was incorporated as a city. In 1810 they had 700. In 1841, 30,000. The rivers above this are more shallow than below & a smaller class of boats are used, so that St. Louis is made a great shipping place & multitudes of steamers are lying here at all times. St. Louis must be the commercial mart for all the north West, as good a section of land as is to be found in the union. There are in Missouri & Iowa valuable mines of lead, copper & coal and also all the products of a temperate climate are raised here in great quantities. This is the depot of the fur traders from the N. W.

St. Louis has good schools & churches & some fine hotels. The "St. Louis University" under the Jesuits, Kemper College of Episcopalians. Two medical schools. A young ladies' school under charge of nuns of Sacred Heart. Two orphan asylums, one Protestant and one under the care of Sisters of Charity.

The city boundaries are five miles on river & one & a half deep but not near all this is occupied.

In proportion to its size St. Louis has some *fine* buildings and money getting is the "all in all" to the people. The "Planters Hotel" is one of the finest hotels in the west and the wants of the guests are well attended to. The building is a plain substantial brick edifice built with a court in the centre and can accomodate about 150 or 200 boarders. The other hotels are passable, some well kept, but as I am unacquainted with them I will not venture a description. This hotel for comfort & convenience will compare well with any of those in our eastern cities & the rooms are in good taste & very commodious. And none can reasonably find fault. The Cathedral situated on Walnut St. is a neat edifice in its exterior & altho not large as well finished and built as any building of its size in the union. Its interior is beautiful & has a very imposing effect. On the opposite side is a description.[35] The building seen in the engraving of St. Louis with the dome is the court house, which when finished will present a fine appearance. It is well located and altho' of singular shape will be a very fine building. As I said in regard to Columbus it is devoutly to be hoped that when St. Louis has finished the repairs on her court house a new era may commence and the law be supreme: as it ever should be in a republican country.

St. Louis has a very large foreign population who exercise a very deleterious effect upon the city. Law is not always powerful, that is *civil law*. Mob law is too frequently exercised. This city has been the theatre of several riots & mobs. At the close of the election this week the quiet of the city was broken by a lawless mob & but a few weeks since the mob came very near destroying the medical college connected

[35] The picture and description facing page 136 were pasted into the diary.

with University owing to the indecent exposure of dead bodies. Where an excitement prevails here against any man or set of men he may as well move or he may hear from "the free & enlightened people." A few years since a negro was burned to death here for murder and many instances of the mob spirit have been exhibited here. For altho in every case wrong may exist yet the law should always be allowed to have its course. The result of this is that sooner or later all those cities having a large foreign population must run "a native American" ticket in opposition to the scapegoats who countenance a mob spirit by means of the lower classes of foreigners & thus corrupt the city government.[36]

In morals St. Louis is of the same school of other river cities and many things are countenanced here which are ruinous to any people. Time & moral & religious efforts will do much to abolish & banish this spirit. For altho men may be deserving of punishment in cases like the gamblers of Vicksburg &c &c yet there is no doubt that in a civil government the law should only be executed by its officers. It is deeply to be regretted that this great valley of the Mississippi should be the theatre of so much vice, sin & immorality, and those who foresee the greatness to which this section must arise should also try to breast this tide of sin & lead men to do right.

The business of St. Louis is very great. The grain, pork & beef of this western country naturally comes here. The min-

[36] Nativism, or the spirit which dictated that emigrants should be deprived of easy methods of naturalization and should be prevented from participating in political activities, had rumbled under the surface for a long time. In 1843 in New York City it had taken the outward form of a political organization which had notable success in the municipal elections of 1844. In New Orleans, too, Whipple may have run into it, for the American Republican Party had, by the autumn of 1844, become a real political factor. In New York the party was called the Native Americans. M. St. P. McConville, *Political Nativism in the State of Maryland, 1830–1860* (Washington, 1928), pp. 1–2; J. D. Hammond, *Political History of the State of New York* (New York, 1848), 3:477–48.

This beautiful building situated on Walnut St. St Louis is one of the best proportioned and built buildings in the west In its exterior it is plain & neat with a portico in front and above it the letters "Deo uni et Trints". On either side in the niches is carved in letters of French and english "My house shall be called the house of prayer" and above the cornish is also "The tabernacle of the lord is with men" written in English French and Latin The buildings seen on each side of the Cathedral are orphans assylums Kept by the sisters of Charity and the nuns of the sacred heart — The children are well taught and clothed and seem happy. By such offices of Kindness the catholic church has a strong hold on the affections of many of the people.

Cathedral, St. Louis
(facsimile of an insert in the original diary)

eral productions of the North West also come here on their way to a distant market and very considerable of this produce is sold here or exchanged for goods. As an evidence of the large amt of produce shipped here "the steamer Missouri on her last trip to New Orleans carried down & towed on the barge over 1700 tons of merchandise. She had over 9000 keg barrels & Hhds., over 6000 pigs of lead and 800 bales of merchandise besides hides &c. She is but one boat of a great number & this is but one trip. But this is sufficient to show what is doing. The only danger is, as the Arkansas folks say, that they will be so eager to do business that "they will run the thing aground." At present the prospects of this city are excellent, and certainly to all human appearances St. Louis must be a great and a prosperous city. There are a great many eastern men here doing business, but unfortunately "the omnipotent cash dollar" has filled so much of their thoughts that they cannot stop to try and stay the tide of sin and bring men back to reason & religion. Mr. Green the reformed gambler has been here & it is hoped he is doing good, but I fear it will be many years before the west is free from this vice—a vice which brings on its infatuated victim certain & sudden ruin. Many a man of bright hopes & a pure character has been ruined for time & for eternity by this pernicious evil. There will be needed a long pull, a strong pull & a pull altogether before it can be checked or allayed. This fairest portion of our country has many plague spots on it which will ruin & destroy unless a cure is effected. May the time soon come when it shall be as fair in morals as it is in natural qualities.

I left St. Louis today April 6, 1844 on the "Goddess of Liberty" for Cincinnati. Our boat altho' bearing the euphonious title of a "goddess" proved anything but a goddess—for never in my life have I seen a boat which professed to be a first class steamer that was so utterly destitute of all comfort and convenience. Instead of quiet and a reasonable number of passengers we had over 300 and such a motley crew of mortals I will wager never before were seen in one boat. My lucky star was in the ascendant, for I fortunately secured a state room with my fellow traveller Mr. Kingman and was thus far provided for. The scenery between here & the mouth is very good indeed, in many places wildly beautiful. The arsenal situated a few miles below St. Louis is the first object of attraction and presents a neat appearance, & its site is well selected as well as that of the powder magazine, which is seen in the distance. The Jefferson Barracks is another beautiful spot & I think the best located of any such government building in the Union. The site is on the top of a hill near the river, and the parade ground shaded by trees & the fine neat buildings make a very pretty view. Kaskaskia, Carondelet & the other small towns are very picturesquely situated and form good views. But the greatest enthusiasm must vanish and so did my delight at gazing on the varied scene and as I descended to the cabin I felt in its full force the horrors of being penned in so small a compass with such a crowd. All conventional forms were set aside. Men smoked in the cabin, spit showers of tobacco juice on the carpet, talked loud, laughed heartily and did every thing as if bent on proving to all that a steamer should be if she was not a bar room. We had H. Russell of N. Y. on board, also a Baptist clergyman, a Mormon elder, Green the Reformed Gambler, and a reasonable number of representatives of all other 'isms—big & little Danl Lamberts[37] & Tom Thumbs, Jack Falstaffs & living skeletons, tall Kentuckians and short pigmies, drunkards, dandies &

[37] Daniel Lambert (1770–1809) weighed 739 pounds when he died.

loafers, oh! such a crew! When the supper bell rang what a rush, one grand race, and woe to the luckless wight who should stop in his course, he might well expect to be crushed to death—and then such a clatter of knives & forks & table ware, such screaming for waiters, such appeals to Bill, Tom, Jack & Pomp & such an exhibition of muscle & nerve as men entered with all their powers into the game of knife & fork. It was worse than a second Babel. As a Missouri "puke" who stood next to me said "it looked for all the world like one great scrimmage." The table was cleared in an amazing short space of time & food was *bolted* as I have never seen before. When the 2ond bell rang another just such a grand rush "only more so." The 3rd table was more quiet, probably because "patience had had her perfect work." Such were our meals. At night the cabin looked like one great hospital, hardly room for a dog to place his foot, so close were they stowed away on the "spoon bill" order. As for the quality of our food, oh! never mention it. It was eat & that is enough.

Sunday morning we had a beautiful sermon from the Baptist elder from the text "they hated me without a cause" and he preached exceedingly well. In the afternoon we had a sermon from the Mormon, a very plain discourse, but very well calculated to mislead the ignorant. This elder is on his way to Europe, the scene of his former labours. I had a long conversation with him on this subject & was much amused by him. Monday we had a lecture from the Reformed Gambler. He is an illiterate gambler, once the worst of men, but now doing all he can to break up this vice. His influence failed to stop it on our boat, for during the week days we had gambling in the cabin constantly. One evening we had a concert, another a lecture, another a ball. The time passed quickly away and none of us felt lonely on the boat altho we all shuddered when the thought of the dreadful results which might result from any accident.

Above the mouth of the Ohio & indeed all the towns between the mouth and Louisville are of no note, altho many of them are beautifully located and are thriving villages who do a good business with the interior and are a credit to their citizens. [Blank in MS.] are among the best of them & New Albany does a good business at steamboat building. Louisville is a city containing 30,000 inhabitants, and has an excellent business. The city was first settled in 1778. In 1788 they had only 70 inhabitants. In 1800 but 600. In 1843 over 28,000. The city is situated just above the Falls of the Ohio, and presents a very fine appearance as you are coming up the river. The bank is here quite high, altho' not steep, and the houses extend entirely to the river. The Falls are not navigable for steamers except at very high water and to obviate this difficulty a canal has been made around them sufficiently large to lock through it steamers 40 feet wide & 180 feet long. But the larger class of boats only come up to the canal. This was considered as one of the greatest undertakings of the age at the time it was commenced, but since completed pays well, as the charges are exorbitant, 50 cents pr ton. The excavation is mostly rock. I here saw the Ky. Giant. He keeps a grocery at the mouth of the locks and is a curiosity, 7 feet 8 inches in his shoes, & he has a gun which is 8 feet long. He seems in bad health. The city of Louisville will not appear to most as beautiful. It is a city of business & not of pleasure. The streets are very regular and of good width. In the back part of the city are some fine residences and shade trees.

The Epis. & Pres. churches are very fine specimens of chaste architecture of the Gothic order, and are well worthy of visiting. The court house now being completed is a mammoth building & of fine proportions but the square tower on its top has spoiled the beauty of the whole. It is said it will cost a million of dollars. It was commenced thus in hopes of transferring the capital of the state to Louisville & making it the state house. They are also completing a new jail, a unique & neat affair of a different style from any I have ever seen. Louisville has some few factories for manufacturing hemp into bale rope & bagging. The wholesale business here is large, and there is also a large forwarding business done here. Louisville has grown very rapidly in a few years and is destined to become a great city. The land around it is rich and generally well improved. Large quantities of tobacco & hemp are shipped from here yearly & besides a good wholesale trade is done here with the interior. The morals of this city are better than most southern cities, altho there are many sporting characters who infest this place, and much sin is thus engendered by these roving gamblers. The people seem desirous to make Louisville what such a city should be in morals and religious character. The schools here are very good altho' not as good as those of Cincinnati.

Louisville has increased in size much within the last few years and is a fine business city. The state of Kentucky is wealthy & prosperous & her valuable lands & agricultural productions form a good basis for believing that this will yet be a large city. As usual Clay is popular here & Prentice of the "Journal" is a team of himself, one of the wittiest & shrewdest men in this section.[38] He has done & is still doing much for

[38] George D. Prentice (1802–70) was born in New London County, Connecticut, and graduated from Brown University in 1823. After working on two New England papers he went to Louisville, where in 1830 he started editing the *Journal* and continued to do so until the merger of that paper with the *Courier*, forming the *Courier-Journal* in 1868; he continued to write editorials for the new combination until his death. He was an early supporter of Garrison but was "wholly subverted

his party. Had an election for president on our boat and Clay had 40 majority.

The scenery between Louisville and Cincinnati is much the same as below. The river is much narrower here than farther down and is skirted by high lofty hills covered with rich green foliage and at their base a wide belt of level table land which makes the scene still more beautiful. Nowhere have I been more delighted in gazing on nature than here. At times you can see miles & miles on the river, and as you look far in the distance, it seems like one long deep ravine: again the river turns so abruptly that you almost fancy we have reached the end and that beyond the bank in front there is no river. I sat hours and hours and gazed around me with joy & delight. The cloud capped hills, the rocky cragged precipice, the beautiful valley, the rich green foliage & the calm, placid river all formed a bright and a glorious landscape. The villages scattered here and there along the banks of the river are beautiful & generally seem thriving.

Today (April 10, 1844) we passed North Bend & our boat stopped for a short time to land some passengers who lived near here. This was the residence of the late President Harrison and is a most beautiful place. Fronting the river is a broad strip of level land & back of this the land rises gradually to the top of a high hill. On the north west side of the house is his grave, nearly ⅛ or ¼ of a mile from the house. His tomb is plainly seen from the river. He is buried on the top of a small hill which rises like a mound from the other hills and this is

to the Slave Power" when he went to Kentucky. See *William Lloyd Garrison: The Story of His Life Told by His Children* (Boston, 1894), 1:183. In his early Kentucky days Prentice engaged in editorial conflict with Shadrach Penn of the *Advertiser;* his wit and satire were copied widely and "even the English journals had each their column headed—'Prenticeana.' " Lewis Collins, *History of Kentucky,* revised by Richard H. Collins (Covington, Kentucky, 1874), 2:363. For a sketch of Prentice see *ibid.,* 2:389–91.

fenced in & surrounded by shade trees. It is a sweet looking place, and one well calculated to suit a man of Gen¹ Harrison's peaceful taste. The house is a two story house, of the plainest style with small additions on each end, and situated in the midst of shade trees. On one corner of the place stands a small log cabin which I suppose has been suffered to remain in memory of 1840 & also of his having been called "the poor man's friend." I was much gratified at seeing this last resting place of a great & good man. Irrespective of its associations it is a beautiful place, but doubly so when its history is known. For all feelings of party sh'd be forgotten when a great man dies & he sh'd be remembered by all our citizens not as a member of a party but as "an American."

(Don't forget the drunkard's story.)[39]

But I see by the grand rush of passengers hither & thither that we are at Cincinnati—and so farewell to our boat, farewell to the acquaintances of today, whom I shall see no more until I meet them at the judgement.

As you near the city the surrounding hills seem more & more beautiful and you are almost enchanted by the wildness & grandeur of the view. The river here turns quite abruptly & at once the "Queen City" appears before you. I must confess, I was disappointed with the place. The high hills seen in the distance back of the city are naked & destitute of foliage in many places, as these hills are dug away to procure limestone for building. The compactness of the houses, the new & fresh appearance of the brick walls & the heavy black smoke from numerous manufactories, all seem to combine in cheating you of the romantic view you had expected. The levee at which you land is broad & deep & affords a fine place for transacting street business & receiving & discharg-

---

[39]Apparently he did, for it does not appear in the journal.

ing cargoes. Below this lie a legion of empty flat boats which tell well for the business of the city for, as "an Arkansas horse" said as we passed them, "folks never build them things for fun." We selected a car man and wended our way to the Henni House where we were glad to cast anchor, and felt thankful that we had been spared on our long & perilous journey. And now adieu my journal until tomorrow. No letters from home. Why don't they write? Why is it? Patience, patience, but it's hard to school one's self against the anxieties we feel for absent friends.

Cincinnati. "The Queen City" was first settled in 1778. In 1800 it had but few inhabitants and was but a quiet country village. In 1812 it was made a city and since that time has rapidly increased until it has become a large & flourishing city. Its present population is over 65,000 inhabitants and it is said that during the past year it has had added to it nearly 1,000 new buildings. The hard times affected its citizens very much and for a time business was stagnated but the city has nearly recovered & business is very flourishing. During the last year some fine steam boats have been built here & many fine buildings erected. *Hog*—is the grand staple of this city, and a man with half an eye might guess the same, by the number of these 4 footed scavengers seen in the streets. About 250,000 hogs were slaughtered here last year and this pork sold here was worth over 1,000,000 of dollars & the flour & whiskey shipped from here was valued at as much more. They have several manufactories here for making lard oil, which is shipped to Europe, West Indies, & diff^t parts of our country. They have also extensive mills, factories, & slaughter houses and on every side of you, you see evidences of the enterprise of its citizens. There are few places of public amusement; a museum and a theatre situated in a beauti-

View of Cincinnati
(from a print found in the original diary)

ful garden are all of note. The churches are numerous, &
their number tell me, I am again in a land comparatively
moral & pure. All denominations are well represented, including, Jews, Mormons, Catholics, Restorationists, Univer-
salists, Disciples, Christians, Episcopalians, Methodists, Baptists, Millerites &c &c to the end of the chapter. Many of
these churches are beautiful & elegantly finished. There are
two or three of the Gothic order which would be an ornament to any city. The new Catholic Cathedral is a massive
structure & when finished will be a splendid building. It is
plain but of neat appearance & of excellent proportions.

The city is blessed with fine schools, and education is
within the reach of all. There are some fine colleges & medical institutions here—Xavier College, medical college, commercial college, Lane Seminary & other similar institutions,
all of which rank well in literary character and are a blessing
& ornament to the city.

The city is situated in a valley, surrounded by high hills
and built partly on the first & partly on the second bank of
the river & then running back to the base of the high hills
on each side. Fronting it is the Ohio River & beautifully does
it look. From the top of Prospect Hill you have an excellent
view of the city & suburbs and it is indeed beautiful. At
your feet is a large and flourishing city, filled with restless,
busy mortals. Around you are a chain of high hills & here &
there deep ravines. On the other side is the Ohio, filled with
water craft and a scene of bustle & noise. The newness of the
houses, the many new buildings being erected all make it
seem almost like enchantment. From this hill are seen all
the streets, gardens, public buildings & manufactories of
Cincinnati & the quiet villages of Covington and Newport

in Ky. The eye sees all at one glance, a valley teeming with its thousands and full of life & activity.

The valley in which this city is situated is about 15 miles in circumference and is divided in its centre by the Ohio. Cincinnati is on the north bank and Newport & Covington on the south bank. Licking River empties into the Ohio here. Cincinnati is destined to rank high as a commercial city. It has great advantages for an inland city, fine McAdam roads, canals & steamboat navigation, and is a healthy city. When it shall have recovered from its embarrassments and money is easy it will increase in a rapid rate. It is called the Queen City & well does it deserve the name.

April 12th Today in company with my friend D. P. Kingman of Boston I left Cincinnati for Newark, Ohio. The route by way of Dayton to Columbus is quite hilly and the land rich beyond description. The Miami Valley may vie in richness with any lands in the New World. It seemed like one rich fertile garden. It almost seemed like enchantment after seeing so much of the poor barren lands of the south. The trees are already putting forth their leaves & nature is arrayed in her loveliest garment of green. The farm houses generally look well & the frequency of small villages with their neat churches makes me feel at home again in the north. This is a McAdam road & you glide along as easily & far pleasanter than on a railroad car. In many places it is one succession of hills, in other places your route lays for miles through a rich valley. We passed through Sharon, Lebanon, Palmyra, Dayton & Springfield. The last two are very flourishing villages, especially Dayton, which is now incorporated as a city and has a population of about 6000 inhabitants. This will make a flourishing city as it is in the midst of one of the finest sections of the state and for the last few years has improved rapidly. We reached Columbus after a 24 hours' ride fatigued and wearied & happy enough to make Columbus a resting place. Columbus is a city of comparatively small business. It has a population of between 5 & 6 thousand. Being the capital of a rich state it is of course invested with more interest than most inland cities. The state house & state offices are old & shabby buildings unworthy of such a state as Ohio. Arrangements were made a few years since to commence building a state house, but owing to a quarrel about changing the capital, it was dropped for the time being. The asylums are substantial & well proportioned buildings & admirably managed (Blind, Deaf & Dumb & Insane). Such institutions are an ornament to any people & espc. when reared by a new state under great embarrassment. The state's prison located here is another institution well conducted & I was much gratified by a visit to it.

Newark April 24. This is a quiet town, finely located in the Licking valley, & of about 3500 inhabitants and doing a good business with the surrounding country. The scenery near here is wild and beautiful, and there are many very pretty drives in the vicinity. About 1½ miles from here is one of those ancient fortifications so common in the west.[40] The marks of it are much more prominent than I could have anticipated. The bank is still in good preservation & is in some places 20 feet high. It is one mile in circumference. In the centre is a well. There is but one entrance. The ditch is still perfect. So ancient is it, that large forest trees have

[40] A circular mound of considerable size, one of the thousands found in Ohio and elsewhere in the Mississippi Valley. G. F. Wright, "Mounds and Earthworks of Ohio," *Ohio Archaeological and Historical Publications,* 1:346 (March, 1888).

grown on the top of the banks since it was built, one I noticed 4 feet through. It is a curiosity, full of interest to the antiquarian. None know its object, none can tell its history. All in reference to it is vain conjecture and imaginary. But of one thing all are convinced, that it was built by a people of different habits & customs from the native Indian. These monuments of other days scattered though the west tell us that this vast country had inhabitants long ere occupied by Indian race.

But adieu to my journal until I reach Cumberland. I dread the long journey. But as it's by stage there is less danger. As an Arkansas man told me on the river "If you upset in a stage coach in a ditch you are thar. But if you run off the track in a railroad car or blow up on a steamer whar are you? You ain't thar no how." So we will hope for the best & prepare for the worst.

April 25th Today I bade adieu to Newark and to my kind friends there for home. We took a small hack from here to Jacktown and there we meet the Columbus & Wheeling stage. The route to Jacktown is as dull as possible & as the road is bad, you creep along at a snail like pace. When we reached this miserable village, we found we were to wait 2 hours for the stage: time to be spent in being gazed at by curious Yankees. And the landlord & his body guard could outvie "a live Yankee" in questions. "From the south, eh?" inquired he. "No!" said I. "From the west?" again he inquired. "No!" I replied & after being bored a few minutes longer, I told him I was from "Adams, Jefferson County, New York, about 10 miles from Sackett's Harbor" &c &c.

We left this place for Wheeling at 1½ o'clock P.M. Our passengers seem a pleasant set of fellows, full of fun & merriment, all being delegates to the Baltimore Whig Convention and the way they talk of & sing about Harry Clay is rather astonishing to a Loco-foco.[41] The land in the south eastern part of Ohio is very rolling land & in many places the hills are very steep. We reached Zanesville for supper & remained here an hour or two, long enough to see the place. Zanesville has a population of about 7000 inhabitants & is a remarkably flourishing place. The water power here is very good and there is quite a good deal of manufacturing done here, besides several large flouring mills. The buildings are very ordinary, and altogether the place is not a handsome one—altho' it appears well from the hills which rise back of it. Soon after leaving this place, it began to rain & we had a succession of violent thundershowers during the night. Never have I heard such terrible peals of thunder & seen such vivid lightening as during this night. Our belief in the safety of stage travelling was somewhat weakened by hearing at Zanesville of two coaches having been upset the day before & many of the passengers badly hurt. The roads being as smooth as a house floor, drivers drive furiously & carelessly. This road is one of the greatest evidences of the enterprise of Americans I have ever seen.[42] It is made of excellent materials & altho' travelled on by hundreds of heavy waggons, stages &c yet it is seldom rough by being cut up, & stages full of passengers can easily make 8 miles per hour.

[41] Loco-foco was the term applied to a radical wing of the Democratic Party in 1836. Apparently Whipple uses the term to designate a Democrat, as distinguished from a Whig, as did many others after the real significance of the split had disappeared.

[42] The National Turnpike or Cumberland Road, the one early object of federal appropriations for internal improvements, was started in 1806 and by 1838 had been constructed as far as Vandalia, Illinois. See A. B. Hulbert, "The Old National Road—The Historic Highway of America," *Ohio Archaelogical and Historical Publications*, 9:405–524 (May, 1901).

Just as we began to grow sleepy and tired, all of a sudden we were startled by a loud crash and we brought up all standing. On examination we found the driver had driven out of the road & had struck a large rock and broke the tongue off. Had we gone a few feet further we should have been upset down a steep bank & perhaps killed. It was a mercy we were no worse situated. But even as we were we were in a bad fix, for we might lose the mail and not be able to reach Baltimore Saturday evening, as we expected, and so it proved. Never did it rain harder than then, and here we were delayed 3 long hours mending the coach, and even when mended we were obliged to drive very slow. We passed Norwich, Cambridge & Washington in the night and of course could not judge of their merits or beauty. We breakfasted at Fairview and passed St. Clairsville about 9½ o'clock. St. C is a place of considerable retail trade & something of a village. From here to Wheeling you pass some very steep hills, one of which is very winding, and in many places the road takes a very short turn where if you went off the bank you would go down 80 or 100 feet. Our tongue to the coach was so poor there was no way to go down but on a run & never have I seen more skill exhibited by a driver than here. We came the 12 miles in one hour and five minutes—and reached Wheeling about 11 o'clock A. M. 26th Apl.

Wheeling is as dirty and smoky a looking place as I have ever seen. The buildings are blackened with coal smoke and altho beautifully situated, yet in appearance it is far from being beautiful. The river is at present very low and none except the lightest class of boats can go up. There is considerable capital invested here in manufacturing and from its locality it has a prosperous country business. I did not go much about town as the small pox is here & prevailing to a very considerable extent. We remained here until 2 o'clock P. M. and took our departure for Cumberland 131 miles distant over the mountains. The first seventy miles of the route is more level than the remainder of the route. But there is a continual succession of hills & valleys the entire distance. We passed a large number of small villages on the road, of which Washington, Brownsville, Uniontown & Southfield are the largest. The first peak of the mountain you ascend is Laurel Hill, 3 miles of continual ascent. On one side rises majestically a high rocky mountain whose top is lost in mist & fog. On the other side is a deep ravine many hundred feet deep, where if by accident you should fall you would be dashed to pieces on the rocks below. The entire hill seemed strewed with flowers, and these delicate spring blossoms look enchanting, half concealed as they are by the laurel & other trees of the kind. The scenery is wildly beautiful, and I have never gazed on any view half so magnificent. Near the top of the hill is a spring of the finest water I ever drank. From the top of the hill you can see miles & miles & nothing to obstruct the view. The deep valleys & lofty hills, the farm houses and settlements seen in the distance, the national road lined with vehicles of all kinds from the coach & four to the heavy waggons with 6 noble Pennsylvania horses. These & ten thousand other things are all seen at a glance & he who cannot enjoy such a scene as this has never learned to love & admire the works of nature & the skill of art.

After leaving this we descend 4 miles and then for 10 or 15 miles it is up hill & down. Then we begin to ascend again & here we have nearly 11 miles continual ascent, altho' very gradual. In this distance this road ascends 1457 feet and this peak, Keyser's Ridge, is about 2800 feet above the ocean. The drivers drive down these hills, Jehu like, on a full run, and now they are so fatigued with extra work that it's necessary for one of the passengers to ride outside to keep them awake. For the last eleven days they have been doing treble work and have had to drive from 30 to 39 miles per day & this too with coaches having from 10 to 12 passengers on each. For the last 10 days they have sent over from 10 to 15 coaches per day besides the regular lines—and so wearied are many of the drivers that they have become perfectly reckless, and are more than half drunk all the time. I never rode as rapidly in my life as I did two of these routes. The last one of 11 miles is one continued hill, and the road here lays through Cumberland Gap, as it is called, and here the scenery is beautiful. The road is near the bottom of a deep valley and near a beautiful stream which dashes impetuously along. Above you on either side are high ranges of mountains which are covered with green foliage and their tops obscured from sight by dense masses of fog. One could gaze on this wild scenery forever and not cease to find new objects of admiration. About 8 miles from Cumberland is a place they call "Braddocks Run" where the road he made winds its way by the side of a quiet stream. In many places you can see the path of the old road still. We cannot know the greatness of that undertaking until we see the rugged path he had to transport his cannon.

We reached Cumberland at 2 o'clock A.M. Sunday morning & here I shall remain until tomorrow. And I am heartily glad that these rugged mountains are past for however we may love their wild scenery, a long journey here cannot fail to weary & fatigue you much. Cumberland is situated in a valley at the foot of the mountains and as all freight going over the mountains is taken from here the place has a very good trade. About 11 years ago they had a very disastrous fire which injured this place greatly. But now it is doing well again. It has a population of about [blank in MS.] and is scattered over a large space. Its buildings are ordinary, plain & substantial, & its hotels are very good. For anyone can appreciate a good hotel after paying 4/ for very miserable dinners at the taverns on the mountain. (On this route they carried Pres. message 230 miles in 23 h. 50 m.)

After spending the Sabbath in this quiet retired village I left today in the cars for Baltimore. I am glad to find that this is a good constructed railroad and with ordinary care one can be safe.[43] When we first started it was a mystery to me how and where we should get out of this valley for we seemed surrounded on all hands by high rocky mountains. This company have had the greatest of obstacles to overcome in building their road, as it is the most crooked road I have ever seen. The road winds its way along the banks of the Potomac for a great distance. At some points the track lies along a steep precipice, again it winds around the rough projection of a mountain, while 200 feet above your heads are rocks piled up in wild confusion as if threatening to destroy you. There is hardly a point on the road but it affords the stranger a fine view. We passed through Hancock, Harper's Ferry & Ellicotts Mills. The scenery near the last two places is most majestic, especially near Harper's Ferry. Here are the U. S. Armories and the quiet little village looks sweetly as you see it in the distance through the long valley before you. There is probably no place in the Union where you can find a more beautiful view. The views of the Monongahela are good at Brownsville, so at Union Town & Cumberland. But none equal to the rich glorious views seen from the railroad track

[43] The Baltimore and Ohio, chartered in 1827, construction of which was begun in July, 1828, put into operation over fourteen miles of track in May, 1830.

near Harper's Ferry. We have about 800 or 1000 passengers on, all bound for the Clay Convention & the way these fellows can sing is a caution. A part of them are from Ky. dressed in their hunting shirts and boots & they skin the Locos hard on songs. I have been very much astonished at the large amount of display & rejoicing which has been carried on by the Whigs since they have declared for Clay. A man ain't half dressed unless he has an ash cane, a Clay hat, a Clay boot, a Clay glove &c &c &c &c. But here we are near to Baltimore & the Whigs are making it thunder with their noise.

"BALTIMORE," "The Monumental city." As I came here in a crowd, and coming too at such a busy time I expected to find a jam but I did not imagine half. After spending half an hour in scolding porters & fighting for my baggage I wended my way to Barnum's City Hotel and oh! what a crowd of all sorts, kinds, sizes & complexions, sober & drunk, noisy & still, dirty & clean loafers, busters, gentlemen, yankees, oh! never did I see such an assembly and amid all you could hear on every side someone singing some Whig song whose words rhymed to the name of Clay & "Dat ole coon" &c &c. I finally succeeded in getting supper. But as for a bed it was as useless to talk of one as to talk of getting to the moon. I bribed the porter to give me a pillow on the sofa and half sleep & half awake I whiled away the night until the cars left for Washington. Bedlam could not equal the merriment & noise of that evening. I spent a part of the evening, as it was moonlight, in seeing the city. The city of Baltimore is regularly laid out at right angles and contains a pop. of over 100,000 inhabitants. It has an extended business with the south and west and for the last few years has done a good business & been increasing rapidly in size. You get a fine view of the Chesapeake Bay from some parts of the city and there are many objects of interest here to a stranger. I was obliged to give them a hasty examination. The main square of the city called Monument Square is a very pretty one and has erected on it a monument commemorating the battle at North Point, 1814.[44] It is a very neat monument. The city exchange hospital & other public buildings are good; better than I expected to find them. Many of the churches are very fine, but I must leave this until I return from Washington.

Tuesday April 30 1844. I arrived this morning in the cars from Baltimore, and am here safe & sound in the capital of the Union.

From the fact that it was the capital of our country I have ever had a great desire to see it. This city was laid out by Gen[l] Washington[45] & in 1800 Congress first began its sessions here. The city is some 30 feet higher than the river Potomac.

The Capitol is the object of greatest curiosity to a stranger. It was commenced in 1793, and was burned down by the British during the last war. The capitol is situated on a small hill and occupies an area of near 25 acres. The first story of the building is plain of heavy proportions & you rise to the second story on either side of the building. The other two stories are of a more elaborate workmanship, being ornamented with Corinthian columns & pilasters. It has two wings, each surmounted by a small dome, while the main building has a very high & splendid dome. The entire length of front is 352 feet, depth of wing 121 feet, east projection & steps 65 feet, west 83 feet. The following are the costs of building. The

[44] North Point was the place of disembarkment of the British land forces in the attack upon Baltimore in September, 1814.

[45] Major Pierre Charles L'Enfant was responsible for the planning of Washington, D. C. President Washington, Thomas Jefferson, and perhaps others had some general ideas which gave L'Enfant a start. W. B. Bryan, *A History of the National Capital* (New York, 1914), 1:105 ff.

north wing cost $480,262.57. South wing $308,808.41. Centre building $957,647.35. The House of Rep. is in the south wing & the Senate Chamber in the north wing. Both of them beautiful rooms, and arranged with much taste. In the House the room is surrounded by 22 marble columns (of beautiful variegated marble) with capitals of white marble. The dome is magnificent & the paintings finely executed. They were done by Benoni. The speaker & clerk of the House are elevated above the level of the floor & back of their seats are some beautiful damask hangings. Above the speaker is a group of statuary representing Liberty & by her side a beautiful eagle, while on the other side is a serpent wound around the shaft of a column. This was executed by Valaperti.[46] On the other side of the house opposite over the entrance is another group representing History recording passing events & the wheel of the car is made a clock. One one side of the speaker is a beautiful portrait of the Marquis Lafayette, the noble friend of Americans, and opposite a portrait of the father of his country, Geo. Washington. The seats of the members are in the area. Each member has a small mahogany desk & arm chair & back of this under the galleries are sofas for the admission of those privileged to enter the house. All in all the room is a good one, and were members less careless where they spit tobacco juice the hall would be a neat one.

The Rotunda is in the main building under the dome and is decidedly the finest part of the Capitol. It was intended that Greenough's monument of Washington shd stand in the centre, but it is in a separate building. The walls of the Rotunda are ornamented with fresco paintings & in niches are fine specimens of sculpture & ornamental stucco work. Here

[46] Valaperti replaced Giovanni Andrei who, with Guiseppe Franzone, had worked on the first capitol building. "Franzone designed the clock and Valaperti the stone eagle in the house." Bryan, *op. cit.,* 2:32n.

are Trumbull's celebrated pictures, the figures as large as life. The first "Declaration of Independence." All of the signers are accurately drawn as large as life & it is a most impressive scene. There is so much solemnity & strong unbending firmness exhibited on every countenance. The picture fills every American heart with American feelings & memory carries him back to the time when in solemn conclave this noble band proclaimed to the world "Liberty or death." I gazed a long time on it & each moment seemed to see new beauty in it. "Surrender of Saratoga" and "Surrender of Cornwallis" are two other beautiful pictures in same size & style: the chagrin of the enemy, their subdued pride, & haughtiness as well as the joy & gladness of our army is well portrayed. The scene is admirable & must be correctly drawn as Col. Trumbull was well acquainted with all the actors in these scenes. "Washington Resigning his Commission" is another most admirable picture. There is a thrilling expression of interest in the face of every man present & also a look of love, of thankfulness, of joy & hallowed peace. Weir's "Embarkation of the Pilgrims" is a most splendid painting, as is also the "Baptism of Pochohontas." In the Embarkation[47] of the Pilgrims you see the quaint old bark "Speedwell," the godly minister & the Puritan fathers. The holy, calm & trusting look of the aged minister of Christ, as he bows in prayer, is a most splendid effort of the painter, as is also the old Bible, the solemn faced father, the neat & tidy mother, the young girl & the boys. The costumes are those of other days & yet so well executed that there is no stiffness in it. This painting will give him immortality if none other.

"The Baptism of Pochohontas," Chapman represents John & Anne Lawton, a youthful pair, the first couple married in

[47] In the handwriting of someone else. "Landing" is crossed out.

157

the province, and there is a happy trusting look on each face, near them Sir Thos. Hale & his standard bearer & a beautiful page. Rev. Alex^r Whitaker by a vase of water ready to baptise the kneeling Indian girl. Pochohontas, a most beautifully formed Indian girl clad in a robe of down. Her sister & young child, two uncles and an Indian brave with an eagle tied & placed on his head. John Rolfe holding an old Bible &c c. This is like the others beautiful and beyond description. Above these are groups of statuary as "Landing of Columbus," "Danl Boone Fighting Indians," "Penn's Treaty," "Pocohontas Saving Smith"—& above these still busts of "Cabot," "Raleigh," "La Salle," "Columbus." In the portico in front is a statue of War by Persico represented as an ancient warrior. Helmet pressed on his brow & his breast covered by an iron corselet, he is leaning on his shield & holding a sword. The determination & fierce lowering look add much to the figure. On the other side of the portico is a statue of peace representing a maiden offering an olive branch. There is a sweet calmness on the face & such a look of innocence & love that you can but be pleased with the features. In the other side of the grounds is a building where is Greenough's celebrated statue of Washington, well executed, but not such as pleases my taste. Over the Portico is a group of statuary representing Justice, Peace & Commerce standing together, and above the door under the Portico is a group of statuary representing Washington being crowned by Victory with a wreath of laurel. Had I time I would love to dwell more fully on the beauty of these different paintings & statuary, espc. Weir's painting of Pilgrims. Words are inadequate to tell the sublimity of the view.

The Senate Chamber is of same form as that of the house and is adorned by columns of Ionic order & support the gallery. The chair of the Vice Pres. is elevated above the floor & is canopied with hangings of red. The seats are like those of the House. In another apartment is the Library, a large elegant room filled with valuable books. There are works here of almost every kind & in every language & there are also some fine busts of distinguished men & portraits of the presidents. The grounds about the Capitol are extensive and beautifully laid out with different kinds of plants, flowers & shrubbery. Front of the east side is a beautiful pond of water, on the west a monumental fountain dedicated to Somers, Caldwell, Decatur, Wadsworth, Dorsey & Israel. It is very well constructed to commemorate the memory of naval heroes. And altho there is an air of neatness and the grounds seem pleasant yet if in the hands of a man of taste vast improvements could be made in their beauty.

The view from the top of the large dome is beautiful indeed. In front of you is Penn. Avenue, nearly a mile in length, crowded with carriages, ladies & men who look like pigmies so high are you elevated. The President's house, Treasury Buildings, Gen¹ Post Office, Insane Hospital, the beautiful Potomac, all these are seen at a glance—and far in the distance you can see Georgetown & Alexandria. The view is as good a one as I have ever seen and the plan of the city is at once seen. It is in reality a "city of immense distances" as it has rightly been called. But nowhere in the Union can a stranger spend a few days more agreeably than here—without the public buildings this place would be wholly destitute of interest.

"Character of House of Representatives." I think no place in the world is better calculated to cure a man of all personal idolatry than a visit to the city of Washington. Had he any veneration for men and love of titles, he will be very apt to lose the last remains of it ere he leaves the city. He will find that the charm of Hon. is lost, and these men having high sounding titles are not only men in form, but less than men in mind in many cases. The close observer in Washington is ashamed of his servants when he sees them. Never have I seen as large a body of men who were called great men who came as far short from deserving the title. Such a lack of dignity, such a lack of courtesy, of politeness, nay more, of common decency can seldom be seen in a body of men who are law makers. Here the order of things is reversed. "The law maker" many times is "the law breaker." "The judges of law" are "the violaters of law." An open insult, a row, blackguardism & vulgarity when exhibited by a member of Congress is no curiosity and instead of expelling such men from the house, the decent members dare not do it. I had expected to see sad sights but I did not conceive half. I expected to find much talent but I certainly see but little exhibited. Some of the members certainly only need long ears & a tail to make their classification among beasts perfect. Now the house is engaged on the tariff bill & have been for weeks & will be for some time to come: the members are all satisfied that if any alteration was made in the House it would be lost in the Senate & yet men prate away like fools to empty seats & sleepy members day after day. "Bunkum" is a great article here. In hearing some of the members I was reminded forcibly of school boys speaking from a form & if the comparison favors either, the boys should have it. There are very few men of fine talent in the House & when you leave the House & see the noble, calm & kind faces exhibited in Trumbull's picture of the first Congress you feel sad at the difference. There are some men here whom I was extremely glad to see. First & foremost, as is the case with all visitors, you look for John Q.

Adams. There he sits on the left of the speaker with his whitened locks and furroughed cheek, his head very bald, and you can but love him with all his faults (& he has few) for his devotion to the country. He has given to the American people a noble example of a president leaving the chair and taking a seat in the House. He is always there, ever in his seat, and he listens to all that is said. If anything new or strange is uttered he is all attention. When animated his eye glistens & his manner is very vehement. His frame is much palsied by age & his hand trembles constantly. His heart must be sad when he sees the disgraceful scene around him. Cave Johnson of Ky. is another remarkable man. He is yclept "the watch dog of the treasury" & "twenty men" from the fact he is ever looking after public money & generally has 20 men vote with him. He is bald headed, looks very excitable and has a careless way of lounging in his seat. Robt. Dale Owen of Ind. is a talented man & as ugly a looking phiz as you ever saw stuck on any man's face. He must be the man whom Yankee Hill described as being "so very homely he was afraid to go out alone after dark." Mr. White of Ky., former speaker of House and lately engaged in a row with Rathbun is a very fine looking man, tall, straight, with high forehead, and looks like a man of energy. He has been & is very popular with the Whigs of the House. McConnell of Alabama, "the house rowdy" as he is called, is a man of splendid talents, but a brute from drinking. Weller of Ohio, Ingersol of Penn., R. D. Davis & Mr. Benton of N. Y., Dr Duncan of O. D., Lewis of Ala., Giddings of O., Linn Boyd of Ky., Stiles of Geo., Williams of Mass., are men most known abroad & perhaps I may speak again of them as well as of other members hereafter.

"Character of Senate." If we feel ashamed of the body in the south wing of the Capitol, we feel equally proud of our

Senate. It is a body of grave and dignified men, men who do not deal in low blackguardism & vile abuse. They are one of the most dignified bodies of men in the world. They look like men, like thinking men, like men of mind & character. As I glanced around, I could but admire them and altho' it may be American egotism, yet I felt happy & proud to see such men here to rule over us. There is here a great variety of talent, men of different minds & some men of little weight of character, but as a whole they are a noble looking body and when a member speaks other listen. Instead of abuse of slander & of vulgarity you see men using courtesy & politeness even to bitter political opponents. I never spent a more pleasant morning than the one I spent in the Senate.

Patent Office. This public building is built after one of the prettiest models I have ever seen. The proportions are excellent and the basement & first story are divided into rooms for the accommodation of the Patent Office, the second story is one entire room 267 x 62 feet and is occupied as National Institute. The Portico is supported by Corinthian columns in double rows, and was designed to be somewhat similar to that of the Parthenon at Athens. The National Institute has been founded but a few years. It was founded as it now exists in 1840. The room occupied for its collections is one of the finest specimens of architecture in the United States. The room is arched over head & supported by heavy marble pillars. There is much here to please the curious & inquiring and even a cursory view of this department will occupy a day. Old relics of antiquity, natural curiosities, valuable presents, treaties, new inventions and ancient works of literature are here gathered together. The geologist can here find specimens of minerals from every part of our globe, specimens of valuable ores, of beautiful stones & singular petrifactions. Here are dis-

played before you the coral from the depths of the ocean &
the cragged rock from the lofty mountain. Also a great
variety of wood brought from distant portions of the globe.
Plants, shrubs, weeds & roots of new varieties, & a herbarium
containing over 10,000 specimens of flowers brought from ex-
ploring expedition, birds of all shapes, colours & sizes from the
beautiful honey bird of South America to the bird of Paradise from India. From the tiny sparrow to the swan & pelican
of Africa. You may see snakes from 2 inches to 8 feet long,
vipers, spiders & crabs in any shape & almost any size. Sea
weed, sponges, corals & reefs. Beasts from the common mouse
to the wild cat & panther, alligators & eagles. Idols from India
& canoes from North western coast, shields, spears, spear
heads, umbrellas, Chinese hats, shoes & parasols, pyramids of
beautiful shells & idols & fragments from Central America.

There are here also some beautiful paintings by the old
masters, as well as a full length likeness of Geo. Washington
and portraits of American Indians, toads & grasshoppers, eggs
& chickens. War & medicine dresses from savage nations,
beautiful fabrics of silk & glass, of gold & purple, of carpets &
horse cloths, some sent with Cashmere shawls to Pres. Van
Buren. A diamond snuff box worth $3500, a gold scabbard &
diamond hilted sword, beautiful sabres & swords. Then here
are exposed the treaties with foreign powers & I saw the signatures of Napoleon Bonaparte, Louis 18th King of France,
of Louis Philippe, of Frederick of Russia, of George 4th of
England, of Don Pedro of Brazil, of Ferdinand of Spain, of
Frederick Wm of Prussia, of Francis 1st of Austria, of Berna-
dotte of Sweden &c &c. Yes, those faded signatures were
penned by men full of daring, full of power, many of whom
now lay hushed in death. Here too are the effects of late Mr.
Smithson of England, and a bottle of attar of roses, of 3 times

the value of gold. Here too are old English muskets & fire locks, sabres & swords, some of which did good service in the Revolution. But of far more value than all these curiosities were a few old relics of a national character. Here is that sacred instrument the Declaration of Independence. It is much faded by time, but oh! how solemnly dear is it to all true Americans. The hands who signed it are gone, the hearts whose bravery achieved our freedom are now pulseless & still. But their memory will live forever & until truth shall cease to be eternal will these hallowed names be remembered. Here is Washington's commission as commander in chief. Oh! how hallowed are those two pieces of paper. Here is Gen¹ Washington's old chair, here is his & Franklin's cane & the sword he wore through the Revolution, bearing date 1757 with the letters G. W. Here is his coat, his vest, his breeches & a piece of his old camp tent with the camp dishes. I almost wept as I gazed on these mementos of our country's father. There are many more curiosities here, such as a model of the Nelson Monument &c &c. Mummies, skulls, a hot house of plants from other parts of the globe, Egyptian curiosities found by Gliddon &c &c. But none can equal in interest the relics of our dear noble father Geo. Washington.

The Patent Office proper is in the basement of the building & in the second story, and none will doubt the ingenuity of "the universal Yankee nation" after he has visited this building. You are astonished by the number of useful inventions. Improvements of every kind in agriculture & mechanics besides inventions for useful & ornamental purposes, steam engines, miniature railroad cars, waggons, coaches, saddles, hats, umbrellas, chairs, sofas, knives, pistols, houses, fences, things for all purposes and in all forms. No room in the world can exhibit more evidences of thought than this. We are called an inventive people but none know how true is the saying until he has carefully examined the Patent Office. You feel rejoiced that such useful inventions are fostered by our government and that talent can generally meet its reward. My journal is too brief to give even a glimpse of these rooms, it would take hours to tell the half. Back of this building is the green house & he who loves flowers can gaze here to his heart's content. There are many beautiful plants, some of great richness brought from foreign lands. All in all this is one of the greatest curiosities in Washington. The building cannot begin to compare in magnificence & splendour with the Capitol but its contents are quite as interesting & give the beholder far more pleasant sensations than do some of the specimens exhibited in the Capitol. Should this National Institute continue prosperous none can tell to what extent it may reach. Already it begins to compete with societies that have existed years in Europe. All who love new & strange sights should spend a day in Washington Patent Office.

The Post Office buildings are most magnificent and the style & perfectness please and delight all. The material is pure white marble on the three fronts & granite for the rear. The style is of the most beautiful Corinthian & Grecian order and the effect of the elegant pilasters & columns on the plain base is splendid. The cornice is heavy & of a plain yet very fine style. This building I think is the best specimen of the style of architecture I have ever seen. It is 264 feet long & sixty five feet wide with two wings one hundred feet long & fifty four feet wide. It has over eighty rooms & is occupied by the General Post Office.

The Treasury Buildings are very extensive, being of size of 457 feet in length by about 80 wide. It is built of dark grey free stone & is of the Grecian order of architecture. There is a splendid colonnade or portico the entire length, supported by heavy pillars and it has a very imposing appearance. The proportions are good & the building is very massive. It has 250 rooms & the corridors are vaulted with beautiful ceilings & with tessalated pavements. This, although less beautiful than the Post Office, is very fine.

The President's house is one mile from the Capitol at the other end of Pennsylvania Avenue & stands on a large plat of land elevated some 50 feet above the river and fronts both north & south. From the south you have a splendid view of the Potomac. The grounds are laid out very finely with shrubbery & forest trees & intersected with broad gravelled walks. The building is built of white free stone & is of the Ionic order with pilasters. It is two stories high & the north front has a spacious portico supported by heavy pillars. As you enter the house you enter a broad splendid hall & opposite the front door is the reception room. The chimney pieces & tables are of black Italian marble and were once no doubt very beautiful, but now they are rusty with age. There are a few articles of present beauty, the two splendid chandeliers, as also the eight splendid pier glasses, but the furniture generally is among the "has beens." The splendid carpet is in threads & tatters & patched in many places with other colours. The chairs are old & generally have ragged covering, so much so that it was necessary to put on them linen covering. The room itself is a magnificent affair, high & spacious, of the Corinthian order with pilasters on the walls. The papering was once a magnificent affair but now looks in some places soiled. The private reception room looks better. Here is a fine portrait of Gen¹ Washington, as also of the family of the President, some of which are beautiful. In one corner sits Gen¹ Harrison's old arm chair which he brought with him from North Bend. Here too some of the chairs are in the same dilapidated state. This is a public shame, a disgrace to the people. A people as rich as we are ought not to allow the president's house to be in such a state as to excite the mirth of foreigners.

The grounds are beautifully laid out with serpentine walks and look charmingly. In front of the northern portico is an extended lawn & in it a circular grass plat & in its centre the statue of Thomas Jefferson done in bronze by a pupil of the celebrated David of Paris. He is represented as standing, holding in one hand the Declaration of Independence & a pen in the other. This Declaration is perfect & has the signature of John Hancock & Th. Jefferson. At his feet is a beautiful wreath on a pile of books. The calm dignified look tells how well the artist executed his trust. Jefferson's character is well portrayed in the statue & it is an ornament to the grounds. The south side of the house is equally beautiful with the north & has a fine circular porch: the whole appearance of the buildings and grounds is very fine, and were the house decently furnished, it would present to the stranger a complete edifice, a residence worthy of him whom the people delighted to honor.

I have spent this afternoon 1st May in examining still further the Capitol & here let me speak of the peculiar excellence of the portrait of Genl Washington which hangs over the speaker's desk. It is a gem of beauty & none can well imagine the mildness of the features & the softness of the paintings. I had also pointed out to me the place where Harrison & Van Buren were inaugurated. I also saw here the model of a beautiful floating dry dock which Mr. Dakin the patentee very kindly explained to me. But the wonder of wonders is

Prof. Morse's electrical telegraph. By this means information can be transmitted with almost the rapidity of thought; the cars where [*sic*] telegraphed & the news of nomination received one hour and a half before they arrived here.[48] The machinery is simple & plain. The telegraph is now in operation 22 miles. Prof. Morse has been engaged 12 years in perfecting this wonderful invention. He gave me a specimen of the writing as well as explained the work. He also held communication with the man at the other end of the route. I never will doubt again the extent of man's inventive powers. The rapidity with which the news travels may be judged by the fact that it goes 180,000 miles a minute—wonderful—wonderful. As an Arkansas man said of it "Wall stranger that jist beats me all up! I never sawed nothing till I saw that." A man might spend weeks in Washington & just begin to see. There is much to please the eye, much novel & curious to investigate, and while I live I shall ever remember with pleasure my visit to Washington.[49]

"Return to Baltimore." Left Washington today at half past four A. M. and expected to see the largest crowd I have ever seen and I was not disappointed. The route of the railroad is pleasant & you see some very pretty views. We passed Bladensburg.[50]

After leaving Baltimore the route is a very pleasant one. You pass through several fine flourishing towns, and you see much beautiful scenery. We passed through Hartford, Havre

[48] This is the statement as it appears in the manuscript. It appears to mean that the telegraphed news and the train from Baltimore started at the same time and the message was received an hour and a half before the "cars" arrived in Washington.

[49] The author leaves spaces on the following page for the topics "Society in Washington," "Political Caucusing Here," and "Slavery," as though he intended to fill them in at some future date.

[50] The author leaves spaces for the topics "Banners &c &c," "Procession," "Devices," "Crowd," "Women," "Coons &c," "Arches & Flowers," and "Canton Indians &c."

de Grace, Elkton, Wilmington, & Chester. At Havre de Grace
we left our cars for a steamer across the beautiful Susque-
hanna. This is one of the loveliest rivers I have ever seen and
the views on it are charming. Wilmington is a very large
flourishing place having a populaton of 10,000 and does a fine
business. It has few fine buildings, none of note. Here we
again left the cars to take steamer for the Quaker City. We
had some pleasant views on the Delaware, which were so
much like some views on the lower part of the Hudson River
that I felt quite as if nearing home. The land on this route
is generally very poor and the niggers are the sorriest specimens of human kind I have ever seen. The soil is a thin one
and owing to bad farming nearly exhausted. Wilmington I
learn from the gazette has a number of manufactories and
owns considerable shipping. The city is supplied with water
from the Brandywine by water works like those of Philadelphia. It has a U. S. arsenal. The flouring business is carried
on very extensively at this place.

Havre de Grace is a very old town & was laid out in 1776,
but has never regained the loss it sustained by being burned
by the British in 1813.

Chester is one of the oldest places in Pennsylvania & was
laid out in 1654 under the name of Upland. It is a very neat
place but of no note whatever. I had pointed out to me the
place where a battle was fought during the Revolutionary
War at a place called Red Bank. Col. Greene commanded the
Americans & Col. Count Dunop the Hessians.

Fort Mifflin is a beautiful fortification to protect Philadelphia. There are very many points on this river where the
scenery is very good. There are a great number of small craft
continually in sight and you are continually passing farm
houses & small villages. It is a very pleasant trip from the

monumental city to the City of Brotherly Love. I rode in the cars with Capt. Young of Philadelphia police, a very companionable man who gave me some chapters in the process of rogue catching. He is a vain man but I suppose is well fitted for his business. This is a great harvest for blacklegs and thieves and a man must look sharp or he may be robbed. Philadelphia appears very beautifully from the river, and I am rejoiced that I am 95 miles nearer my home than I was this morning. But one week more & I can enjoy a little calm and quiet & not be doomed to be jaded from pillar to post as I have been for the last six months. Here we are at the wharf amid the usual number of cabmen, carmen, thieves & porters.

Philadelphia is I think far the most beautiful large city I have seen since I left home. It is very regularly laid out and the streets are generally of good width. It has a population of over 270,000. There is no city in the Union more celebrated for its superior literary institutions and excellent societies for benevolent purposes. There are here many objects of great interest to the stranger & first of all "the old state house." This building is of a rather old style built of brick but of itself, aside from local recollections, is of no kind of interest. The exterior of the building has been repaired but much of the old work still remains. The room where the Declaration of Independence was signed is still almost entirely in the same state as when occupied by those noble men. A few years since this old panelling & ornamental work was taken out and the room fitted up in the new style but the people were so dissatisfied that they at once had it altered and the old woodwork was replaced. Two of the same old chairs are there still. In one end of the room is a facsimile of the Declaration—& in front of it a fine piece of sculpture representing Washington. Here is a beautiful portrait of Wm Penn and of Washington &

Lafayette and also one of West's paintings, a magnificent painting of Barnabas & Paul preaching at Lystra. I remained here some time & tried to fancy the solemn scene once enacted here, wondered where sat Hancock, Jefferson &c. Oh! how sacred should this room be kept. Here it was that a band of men assembled such as the world never saw before & never will again. Hallowed be their memory & may each American as he leaves that room leave behind him his self and have that pure love of country which they possessed.

Franklin Library was the next place I visited & it is another spot which all who venerate the name should visit. They have here 55,000 volumes and the rooms are ornamented with maps, paintings & busts of distinguished men. In one corner is a very antique clock, said to have once been the property of Oliver Cromwell. It is a relic indeed. This library shows to all that any man can become educated in a free country & also shows what patience can perform. Such an assemblage of books of all kinds, qualities, sizes & ages I have never seen. Many of them are relics for their age. Here are some of the oldest newspapers—a copy of original rules &c &c &c. All should visit this library & if rightly considered the word "cannot" will be forever blotted from their vocabulary. "The dead monster" was the next place I visited. It is an immense building, and for pure style & proportion unequalled. It is plain & massive, the material is white marble and it fronts on two streets having an elegant portico on each front. At present it is unoccupied & it is said the Catholics are anxious to purchase it for a church. It ought to be purchased by the government for a custom house. It cost the enormous sum of $500,000 but for the kind of edifice is unequalled. It is lamentable to see such a building as this unoccupied & desolate. Back of the state house and in front of Franklin Library is a most beautiful square called Independence Square. It is filled with beautiful plants and shade trees and is a delightful place to walk in during warm weather. There are many such squares in the city, the principal ones are Franklin, Independence & Washington.

I think there is no city of its size in the world that presents a more beautiful variety of shade trees in the streets and public squares. And by the abundance of water the streets are kept neat and clean. "The Water Works" at Fairmount are very fine. A dam has been thrown across the Schuylkill to shut out the tide & by means of heavy forcing pumps the water is forced into an immense pond upon the top of Fairmount; this hill is mostly of rock and the scenery immediately on the banks of the river is beautiful. The forcing pumps are kept in motion by the water wheel, and I think the power is as great as I have ever seen. The garden & banks are ornamented by some very neat & appropriate pieces of sculpture & the grounds are in fine order. The height of this hill is sufficient to send the water over the entire city and in cases of fire water is always abundant. The view from the top of Fairmount of the city is very fine. Near here is the celebrated "Schuylkill wire suspension bridge" one of the most perfect in the country. It is extremely simple & yet immensely strong. The wires are made into heavy ropes by means of bands, and are very strong. It presents a very fine appearance at a little distance. Near here, too, were several small engagements fought with the British. Here are the Gas Works, a very fine establishment and with great facilities in their business.

"The Girard College" as far as completed is one of the finest structures in the Union. But as usual in all such cases money has been profusely squandered & now they lack the means for finishing it. It is a massive structure with a splendid

colonnade around it supported by 36 immense marble columns. The building is fire proof and the chambers & ceilings
are arched in a fine manner. The cornice is elaborate & finely
carved. The professors' rooms near the main building are
plain but of very neat appearance. I was much gratified with
my visit to this elegant & immense building and regret that it
were not finished to go into operation. The donor Stephen
Girard was a very eccentric man & in his will he stipulated
that no clergyman should ever enter it even to see the buildings. The main building is 110 by 160 feet, three stories high &
built of fine white marble. The appearance of the building is
very imposing & the whole is unequalled in the United States.
Mr. Girard left two millions to build it.

The United States Mint is a large & spacious building of a
plain Ionic style but as I had seen the one at New Orleans I
did not visit it. It is said to be built on a very excellent plan.

In passing from Fairmount to Girard College I passed the
Eastern Penitentiary, the finest building of the kind I have
ever seen. It is built in Gothic style to resemble a fort. At each
corner are towers of Gothic style & the doorway has on either
side similar towers which present a beautiful front & has the
aspect of being impregnable. No one can look on this building
without having called to mind the middle ages. But a little
distance from here is the House of Refuge, a coarse substantial
building, and has indeed the aspect of a prison for it almost
makes a man sad to see even its walls.

But the most beautiful place I visited is the Laurel Hill
Cemetery, the home of the dead. The grounds are beautifully
laid out and every necessary expense has been incurred to
make this last resting place of the dead a beautiful spot. The
gateway is elaborate & on either side are lodges in front of
which are colonnades supported by small Corinthian col-

umns, as well as the gateway. The paths are lined with beautiful shrubs & flowers and on every grave some sweet flower blooms to tell of a kind remembrance of the dead. In front of the gateway is a group of statuary executed by Thom of Scotland representing Sir Walter Scott & Old Mortality. The design & execution is excellent and cannot fail to please and gratify the beholder. Here too is a chapel, mansion & other buildings to accommodate funerals. The tombs & monuments are numerous and many of them fine. But lovelier than all are the sweet flowers which bloom on their grave. Back of the hill winds gracefully along the beautiful river Schuylkill. Such a spot as this softens down the gloom attached to death & I believe a visit here is calculated to call forth in every man's heart the nobler & the better feelings of his nature. If he has any love of friends, any social feelings, any reverence for friends dead & gone, these will be called out by a visit to this sweet & hallowed spot.

This custom of having cemeteries like that of Laurel Hill appears to be gaining ground in the country and I think it has a most excellent effect, for it destroys much of that dread which is usually felt at the thought of the grave. The days of terror connected with the graveyard is past and children are no longer learned sad & fearful stories of ghosts and witches, but on the contrary the grave is regarded as a hallowed and cherished spot, a spot around which sweet memories linger & a spot too we delight to visit, and in memory with the past hold sweet communion with the departed. Laurel Hill is much more the work of art than Mount Auburn near Boston. It is less wild & the scenery less majestic but all art can do has been done to make it a sweet and hallowed spot worthy of being the last resting place of the dead. None will visit Laurel Hill & not go away delighted with their visit.

The Navy Yard at Philadelphia is a very good one, although very far from being equal to that at Charlestown, Mass. The buildings are not as good, nor are the grounds as well laid out. At present there is but little ship building here. They have in the stocks a sloop of war to be christened "Germantown." I saw at the foundry near here the celebrated Stockton Guns. It is a wonderful thing that that gun should have burst as it did.[51] The iron looks well & seems strong. They are massive affairs and show to what extent these new inventions are fitted for the work of death. The Princeton, which lies at the navy yard, is the most beautiful vessel I ever saw.

Churches. Philadelphia has many churches embracing all styles of architecture from the most beautiful to the most plain and represent as many different denominations. Some of these churches are very old. The Catholics & Episcopalians have some beautiful churches & they are models for purity & neatness of style. These church spires seem grateful to one's feelings after having been many months in a land of comparatively few churches & great irreligion. I love to gaze on these temples of worship, for they speak well of the people & their morality.

Theatres. There are several theatres here, some of them good edifices, but I am happy to hear that here as well as in most northern cities these receptacles of vice are losing caste & meet with very poor encouragement. Were there no theatres in New Orleans the morals of that place would be far better. Instead of being schools of virtue, they are highways to destruction & infamy.

[51] A reference to the explosion of a new gun on the U. S. S. *Princeton*. Commodore Stockton had invited a large group of Washington dignitaries to inspect the vessel, which was fitted with a screw propeller and mounted two "great guns." On February 28, 1843, the vessel proceeded down the Potomac to below Mount Vernon;

Hospitals. There are many hospitals & benevolent institutions for benevolent purposes here, and all present a good appearance. Many of them are founded by private beneficence, others are public institutions. I saw several of them & was much gratified by their neat & excellent appearance.

Appearance of citizens. The citizens of Philadelphia exhibit as great variety in appearance, as far as dress is concerned, as any city in the Union. You see great numbers of staid plain Quakers & multitudes of dashy genteel fashionables. The contrast exhibited is striking. There is much fashion here & a great deal of display is daily seen in Chestnut St.

Stores. The stores for retail trade exhibit a most elegant appearance & very many of them have pretty girls to tend them. This feature of trade here is unlike any other city in the Union, and a stranger at once notices it.

Hotels. The hotels of Philadelphia are numerous and very good altho none of the buildings are as fine as in most large cities. The American is, I think, as well kept a house as any in the United States.

Markets. The citizens of Penn's City may well be proud of their excellent markets for they are not surpassed in the Union. On market days you cannot avoid being pleased at the excellence of the market, as well as of the good order & regularity displayed in & about it. Generally provisions are reasonably low for a city. I was much gratified with the short visit I made to a Philadelphia market.

Suburbs. The country about Philadelphia is most beautiful in every direction and abounds in elegant and neat country residences. The road to Laurel Hill three miles from the city

occasionally the guns were discharged. On the return trip one more discharge was made, and this time one of the guns burst and killed five of the guests, including Secretary of State Abel Upshur, Secretary of the Navy T. W. Gilmer, and Commodore Kennon. Senator Benton, who was one of the guests, tells the tale in his *Thirty Years' View* (New York, 1854), 2:567–69.

is lined with elegant residences & the grounds are beautifully laid out.

Local Recollections. I enjoyed my visit here more than in any place I have been from the fact that there are so many thrilling Revolutionary memories connected with the city. This was the theatre of many exciting scenes in our Revolution.

Exchange & City Buildings. The city exchange is a very fine granite building, but not as magnificent as that of New York. The rotunda has some fine painting in fresco executed by an Italian artist. I do not like the style of the building altho its proportions are good. The other city buildings are very good but of no interest always excepting those of Revolutionary memory. The banks, as is usual with all buildings built with the people's money, are fine edifices.

Academy of Fine Arts. I spent a few hours here in examining the paintings and statuary exhibited here and was much pleased with my visit to this instituton. Here are some beautiful paintings by the old masters, but the most interesing of all are four paintings representing Human Life. Words are inadequate to express the beauty of them. There are also many superior paintings here by Sully, Inman & other distinguished painters. Two pieces of sculpture representing Bacchus are very fine. There is also an elegant piece of mosaic. The group of Centaurs is very fine and is an object of interest. This room has many fine paintings & all strangers will be pleased with a visit to it.

Fire Department—or as Neal says, "The boys who run with the engine." I saw several of these companies and I will say of them that they are almost "Lusus naturae," for such dirty miserable loafers I have seldom seen & espc. attached to a company formed for the protection of the city. A fire is always followed by a row and a fight, jealousy & rivalry exist to such an extent between these companies that, as the "Pic" says, "a fight follows a fire in Philadelphia with the same regularity & almost with the rapidity" which thunder follows lightening. There are here as well as in most cities a large foreign population, who are a curse to the city. They are engaged in mobs & riots & during elections go with the party that panders to their taste. Philadelphia is cursed as well as all such cities by this poor house scum from other nations & I shall delight to see it done away by the Native American Party.

Philadelphia is a very gay fashionable city, a city full of interest to the stranger & one where the time can be spent profitably as well as pleasantly. My visit here has been very interesting indeed & I should delight to remain here longer examining it & its curiosities.

The diary ends here.

The following section includes miscellaneous bits of information of special interest to the author recorded by him at the end of the journal proper, as well as descriptions of the prints inserted in the original diary.

SLAVE LAWS IN GEORGIA

A part of the slave laws in Georgia showing a few of the regulations on this subject.

Slave descent follows the mother in condition.

Every free slave must have a guardian.

If a slave is found away from the plantation where he resides or out of the limits of the town where he belongs without a pass he may be whipped 20 lashes.

If he refuses to be examined by any white person in reference to such pass he may be moderately flogged.

Evidence of one negro allowed against another in cases of crime.

One slave teaching another a knowledge of poisonous herbs or other poison shall die as a felon.

If a negro slave shall presume to strike any white man he shall for the first offence be subject to such punishment as the justice shall decree, not extending to life & limb. For the 2d offence death. But if he grievously wound, maim or bruise such person he shall die.

It is not lawful for any slave to buy, sell, traffic or deal in any goods or to keep any boat or raise any horses or cattle & they are liable to be seized by any person & delivered to justice & sold for the public good, except where a pass is given giving such slave permission to sell.

Slave not permitted to rent any house—& person renting to them fined 20 $ [?].

Men slaves exceeding seven not to travel in any highway without a white person. Penalty 20 lashes.

Any person teaching any slave negro or person of color to read or write either written or printed shall be guilty of a misdemeanor & shall be punished by fine or imprisonment in county jail or both.

Insurrection, or attempt to excite it, poisoning or attempting it, committing a rape or attempting it on a white female, assaulting a white person with intent to murder or with weapon liable to kill, burglary or arson & murder of another slave are punishable with death. Any free person assisting or enticing a slave to run away is to be confined to hard labour in the penitentiary one year & then sold for a slave during his life time.

If any person trades with a negro without a pass he may be punished by fine not exceeding $500 or by imprisonment not exceeding six months.

Any person circulating or aiding or assisting in circulating any written or printed paper for purpose of exciting insurrection, conspiracy or revolt or resistance shall be punished with death.

Kidnapping not less than 4 nor more than 7 years.

Importation of slaves prohibited. 1 & not over 4 years and $500.

Harboring a slave, fine of value of slave or imprisonment or both.

Unprovoked beating of a slave, except by owner, overseer or employer by fine & imprisonment.

Cruel treatment of masters by unnecessary & excessive whipping, by witholding proper food & clothing, by requiring greater labour than such slaves can perform, by fine or imprisonment or both.

All wills & contracts of manumission void & all persons making or concerned in such wills or contracts fined $1000.

Person of color not to be employed in a drug store.

It is not lawful for any free person of colour to come into the state (except seamen), fine $100.

Vessels coming here with free blacks subject to 40 days quarantine.

Negro preachers licensed.

No free person of color can be trusted but by a written order from his guardian.

No male slave can be brought from a non slave holding state here—fine and imprisonment.

Every free person of color has to be registered.

Slaves not allowed to work in a printing office.

Pedlars trading with slaves without in the presence of his master fine $100.[52]

[52]The author has left spaces for the topics "Route to New York," "General Reflections on Morals &c," "General Reflections on Business &c," "General Remarks on Character &c," "General Reflections on Liberalism &c," "General Remarks on Agriculture &c," and "Remarks on Slavery." He has also included a list of the passengers on the *Lancashire*.

ACCOUNTS OF STATE LANDS

A short a/c of Florida & Florida lands as given to me by Dʳ Burns of the United States army.

Climate. The climate of east Florida is finer than any other portion of the Union. It resembles the climate of Italy, only is free from the damp unwholesome air so common there during some months of the year. In the southern part of Florida frost is unknown and there are only a few nights in the year at St. Augustine when ice can be found of the thickness of a quarter of a dollar. The winter weather is fine & resembles "Indian Summer" at the north except that in Florida the sky is clear & the air free from the dampness & humidity of the season at the north. The summer is not as oppressive as at the north. The air is dry & you have constantly a fine Atlantic breeze on the easterly side & on the westerly side from the Gulf of Mexico. The people are free from the dangerous fevers of the north & middle states & many of the southern. The extreme dryness of the atmosphere causes vegetable decomposition to dry up before it reaches the putrifying stage. And the sandy soil absorbs dampness so that the surface of the earth is never damp any length of time. Consumption, pleurisy, sore throat & rheumatism are unknown as diseases of the country. In the interior on the banks of the St. Johns & elsewhere the climate is delightful. It resembles that of Cuba. Pilatka is one of the best locations for an invalid in the South. The bilious & intermittent fevers are less dangerous than in most of the southern states and in fact all the local fevers are less difficult to manage. The water of St. Augustine is said to be healthy altho very unpleasant to a stranger. The water of the interior is for the most part cooler & more like the soft water of the northern states. Yellow fever is unknown here except when imported from other places. The strong bracing air of St. Augustine is sometimes too bracing for the consumptive but on the St. Johns the climate is delightful in the extreme, and very soothing to the lungs. The weather is generally dry & would undoubtedly be oppressive except for the winds of the Atlantic & the Gulf of Mexico. On a/c of its delightful climate the planter has a decided advantage here over any other portion of the United States, his slaves are healthier & require less care to preserve their health. Fish & game abound & one could live here forever and dream away his existence as if he were indeed in Mahommed's several paradise.

Soil. There is a larger proportion of productive lands in Florida than in any of the southern states. One reason for this is that the tropical climate causes even inferior lands to yield valuable productions. The greater proportion of lands are pine lands. Divided by Dr Burns into 3 classes. The first rate pine land is covered for 5 to 6 inches deep with a dark vegetable mould beneath which is a chocolate colored loam mixed with lime stone pebbles & resting on a substratum of clay & limestone rock. The durability of this land is established from the fact that for 14 successive years it has raised 400lb sea island cotton to the acre & is not exhausted. The second rate pine lands form the greater proportion of available Florida lands. They are heavily timbered with yellow pine, generally high, well watered and healthy. They will when cow penned produce 1200lb sugar to acre. They can also be made to produce tobacco, oranges, lemons, limes & other tropical productions. The third rate lands are not worthless. They are of two kinds, one high, rolling, sandy districts suitable to raising local hemp & the other low, flat, wet lands affording pasturage for cattle &c. The best lands in Florida are first the swamp lands, second the low hammocks, third the high hammocks & fourth the first rate oak & hickory lands. The swamp lands are the most durable lands. They are of recent formation & occupy natural depressions or basins which have been filled up with vegetable matter washed in from the higher lands & when properly ditched they are inexhaustible. Near New Smyrna 4 hhds of sugar was raised to the acre. The land is much like west Louisiana lands, only here they have an advantage on a/c of climate. There the cane has to be cut in October & November on a/c of frost while here the crop can mature till December—& beside this the low hammock lands lie near sandy lands & can be thus tilled while the owner can live in health. Low hammocks yclept "swammocks" are not inferior to swamp lands in fertility but are far less durable. They are always level & the soil is deep & well adapted to cane. High hammocks are lands in best repute in Florida. They are high & generally undulating. They are formed of vegetable mould mixed with sandy loam—and is exceedingly fertile & is generally healthy. The oak & hickory lands are numerous & are much easier cleared than hammock lands & preferred by small planters. Manure is easily procured from swamp grass

& marl. The timber in hammock lands is valuable live oak, red cedar, cypress, hickory, magnolia, wild orange, cherry, mulberry. Mr. Chazzote of St. Domingo says that in the south of Florida coffee, cocoa, indigo &c & can be raised as well as in the West Indies. An acre of 2^d rate pine lands "well cow-penned" will yield 1200^lb of sugar which at 5^c is $60.00. In the same way improved it will yield a crop of 300^lb sea island cotton. And one acre of this land yielded 1800 dollars culti-vated in oranges—most parts of the good lands of east Florida are well calculated to produce sea island cotton. The climate of Florida will not admit of corn being planted so close as at the north but 2 crops can be raised in one season. Pine apples, arrow root, olives, grapes &c &c can be raised here easily & all of the vegetables of the north. You can also raise two crops of potatoes in one year, one of Irish by plant-ing in January & the other in July of sweet potatoes.

Dr Burns ridicules the idea that insects such as mosquitoes are any more numerous in Florida than in the other states & believes the reports of their remarkable size & powers of offensive war are fabulous. He is unwilling to believe the story of the worthy who fishing on the St. Johns said he had occasion to lay down & covered his head with a kettle so as to avoid them & buried the rest of his body in the sand, but to his surprise they bored a hole through the kettle & stung him & his head swelled up so large that he wore the pot some weeks before his head reduced itself so as to remove it. Neither does he believe the story that they carry brick bats under their wings to sharpen their bills on. Alligators abound in the rivers & lakes & are more numerous than in any other section of the country. Doubtless this excellent climate renders the lands of Florida more productive than they otherwise would be yet I am satisfied that Dr Burns has spread the plaster too large & most persons will be disappointed at visiting Florida. For undoubtedly the larger proportion of Florida land is unavailable, either from sickness or poorness of soil—altho' there are many beautiful tracts of rich arable land healthy as well as fertile. Population in 1840 54,477 of which 25,300 slaves.

Georgia Lands and Climate. The lands of the low country of Georgia are of a sandy nature much like the sandy lands of Florida. If properly cultivated and manured they produce very well the great staples of the country but this class of land must be very exhaustible & the plan of most planters is to exhaust land as soon as possible and move on to new lands. There are some small patches of hammock lands and these are of a rich and durable nature. Beside these lands there are the swamp lands on the banks of the rivers and where these can be properly drained they make inexhaustible lands. The rich rice lands of Georgia are of this nature. The lands of the upper country are more clayey and are stronger than the poor pine lands of the low country. The climate of the low country of Georgia is delightful altho' there are many sudden changes in places affected by the sea air. The climate of the up country is much cooler and is not considered as good for invalids with pulmonary complaints as the milder climate of the low country. I saw green peas on the table in Georgia Christmas with beans, radishes & other garden vegetables. The up country lands are capable of producing large crops, and especially in the Cherokee country there is much good land. In the mountainous districts some gold mines have been discovered which have yielded to their owners a very good profit. The timber of the low country is generally pine, cyprus & some oak, of the up country ash, beech, white maple

&c &c, showing a very diff^t soil. 1840 pop. 691,392 of which 280,944 were slaves.

Alabama Land. This is I should think a very rich state in land. The soil is generally clayey approaching to a loam. The bottom lands on the rivers are excellent & inexhaustible. The pine lands, sandy, are much like those of Georgia similarly situated. On the whole I am better pleased with Alabama land and think it a richer soil & more durable than that of Carolina or Georgia. There is more hard timbered land & the land is capable of bearing better crops. This is a new state & as yet its resources are but little developed.

There is some very fine prairie land in this state and this land is generally very valuable altho' there is much of it that is not as rich as the best western prairie land. The clay land is peculiar to this kind of land for I do not recollect having seen any land that is as decidedly a clay soil & yet so much like a loam as the clay land of some sections of Alabama. This land would in the hands of good farmers with sufficient manure make almost an Eden. But unfortunately southern planters exhaust the land and then buy more, a plan which for the present is prosperous, but in the end proves ruinous to the country. The land is generally well watered & timbered, oak, hickory, beech, maple & other hard woods are found here together with plenty of cyprus, pine willow &c &c. There is not much waste land in Alabama. The great staple of Alabama is cotton. There is a large tract of barren sandy land in the southern part of the state and much piny wood land in other sections interspersed with a very rich soil capable of producing any produce. Pop. in 1840, 590,756 of which 253,-532 were slaves.

Louisiania Lands. There is more waste land in Louisiania than in any state in the Union. Large ponds, lakes & swamps cover much of the surface of the state and are totally value-less. The best lands are the river bottom lands & similar lands located on bayous and small streams, these lands are inexhaustible & very valuable in raising of sugar. In the upper part of the state there are vast tracts of prairie land covered with a thin loamy soil & a substratum of sand. These tracts of land are covered with grass and afford fine ranges for cattle and I am told it is not uncommon to find farmers with 3000 head of cattle and some of these same backwoods farmers are so lazy they have not enough milk to use on the table, with all their wealth in cattle kind. This prairie soil altho' a piny woods, sandy soil, might be made exceedingly valuable if farmers and planters would turn their attention to the enriching of the land. The great staple of Louisiania is sugar and so large are many of these sugar plantations that the crop of a single year has brought the owner $30,000. Cotton is also raised here to a considerable extent but the great staple of Louisiania is sugar. They raise some rice here but in not large quantities. The lands in the southwest of the state are swampy with some few small barren prairies. In the northern part undulating & has a good growth of oak, hickory, magnolia, walnut & pine. In the northwestern part there are many lakes & ponds and the bottom lands on all the rivers & bayous are immensely fertile. Pop. 352,411 of which 168,452 are slaves in 1840.

Mississippi Lands. There has been a bad opinion abroad about this state & owing to the wildness of society & the bad state of public morals the tide of emigration to this state has been limited for some years. The southern part of this state is mostly a sandy country covered with pine with here and there cypress swamps & a few open prairies of some small ridges of undulating land. This part of the state is considered middling healthy & cotton, sugar & other southern production are readily grown here. The northern part of the state is more elevated, the surface of the country is undulating, with bluffs & back of these fine elevated table land. Here you find much soil of a deep rich mould & the country is healthy. The Mississippi borders on this state nearly 700 miles. Peaches, apples, figs & oranges are raised in the difft parts of the state. The indebtedness of the state & the course pursued in reference thereto has made this state unpopular with most of the states. In 1840 the population was 375,651; of these 195,211 were slaves. The state was first settled in 1716 where the city of Natchez now stands & 1817 admitted to the Union. It has no seaport town of any consequence and only 60 miles sea coast.

Arkansas Lands. These lands are held in high repute in the south. The lands which border on Mississippi are much of them swampy & well timbered. In the middle of the state hilly & broken. The state has all kinds of soil, some of the very poorest and on the rivers some of the richest. There are many prairies, but on a/c of the absence of water they are but little sought after. In the western part it is mountainous. The staple is corn & cotton. It is expected that on the borders of its rivers there will be an exceedingly fine tract of cotton land but most of the state is too cold to grow this staple well. In some parts of the state fine mines have been found. The time must soon come when these lands will be much esteemed. Pop. in 1840 97,574, of which are slaves 19,935. In the interior of the state are some hot springs of great celebrity. Admitted to the Union in 1836 and settled.

Tennessee Lands. This is considered a good state of land & very healthy. The Cumberland mountains run through the middle of the state, dividing it into East & West Tennessee.

The western districts are exceedingly fertile of a rich black loamy soil. In the middle are also some fine lands. Hickory, walnut, oak & maple, beach &c grow here in abundance. In the eastern districts and in the uplands of the northern part the soil approaches a clay & is less fertile but affords a very fine range of pasturage for hogs, sheep, horses & cattle which are sent to market in the south & east. Cotton in the southern & tobacco in the northern are the great staples. The cotton is of an inferior quality. The western part is level, the others hilly, mountainous or undulating. There are some salt springs & many mineral productions. In 1840 the pop. was 829,210 of which 183,059 were slaves. Admitted to Union in 1796 and settled in 1757.

Kentucky Lands. The staples of this fine state are wheat, hemp & tobacco. The south eastern part of the state is mountainous & this section of the state is very hilly—immediately near the Ohio River the land is broken for 15 or 20 miles back. The bottom lands overflowed by the river are very fertile. In the interior of the state is a fine tract of land called the "gardens of Ky." from the fine soil. The banks of the Kentucky River are precipitous & the land back from it is very good. There is much upland here well adapted to raising hogs, cattle &c &c. It has some salt springs & mineral productions & some remarkable caves. Its population 1840 779,828 of which 182,258 slaves.

Missouri Lands. On the margin of the rivers are good bottom lands, above these rocky ridges & barren land. In the interior you find every kind & variety of land from the poorest to the best. A great variety of mineral productions. Tobacco, corn &c are raised here. The pop. in 1840 was 383,702 of which 58,240 were slaves. Admitted to Union in 1821.

Illinois, Indiana, Lands on Ohio &c. The land bordering

it is hilly. The remainder of the state is generally level. Bordering the streams are rich bottom lands not surpassed for fertility in the world. Illinois lands & Ohio are much alike in character when similarly situated. But these lands are so well known that it is useless to describe them.[53]

[53] The author leaves space for the following subjects, "Pennsylvania Lands," "Virginia Lands," "Maryland Lands," & "Delaware Lands."

DESCRIPTIONS OF PRINTS INSERTED
IN THE ORIGINAL DIARY

This beautiful building situated on Walnut St., St. Louis, is one of the best proportioned and built buildings in the west. In its exterior it is plain & neat with a portico in front and above it the letters "Deo uni et Trinto."[54] On either side in the niches is carved in letters of French and English, "My house shall be called the house of prayer" and above the cornice is also "The tabernacle of the lord is with men" written in English, French and Latin. The buildings seen on each side of the cathedral are orphans' asylums kept by the Sisters of Charity and the nuns of the Sacred Heart. The children are well taught and clothed and seem happy. By such offices of kindness the Catholic church has a strong hold on the affections of many of the people. The interior of the cathedral is much finer than its exterior. It is neatly & elegantly finished and must have cost the Catholic chuch a large sum of money. The walls are painted in fresco and well done. The roof is arched and supported by heavy pillars stuccoed & painted to resemble Italian marble. The gallery

[54] The engraving shows the word to be "Trino." A facsimile of this print, the only insert with description that would bear reproduction, faces page 136.

for the organ & the recesses underneath are of the same plain style of building. The back part of the church over the altar is very well arranged. On either side are false Corinthian pillars and in the centre near the top a beautiful transparency representing a dove surrounded by cherubs & angels. On either side of the altar are recesses for figures of our Saviour and the Virgin and the candles and flowers so profusely displayed looked very fine. There are hung on the walls some fine paintings of scriptural subjects with many more which are miserably executed. The Catholic church here is wealthy and among its ministers are some men of talent. This evening at vespers I saw the bishop and some dozen or two of the priests & witnessed the service. Among all their faults & errors, the Catholic church has many devoted men.

The above is a very correct view of the St. Charles Exchange & Verandah opposite. The St. Charles is decidedly the best and largest hotel in the United States. It is a small world of itself—a village. In appearance an exemplification of the doctrine of Fourierism. It is capable of accommodating 800 boarders, a population as large as that of Adams. The tables are loaded with the luxuries of a tropical clime & the proprietors are polite & attentive to their guests. Once a week the proprietors give a large soiree & at such times you can see fine dancing, hear good music & finish by partaking of a splendid supper.

The appearance of the hotel by moonlight is beautiful & the imposing appearance of this massive structure with its faultless proportions is beautiful in the extreme. The dome & portico are in fine taste & add greatly to the beauty of the building. A very great variety of character is of course seen

here. From the dandy, with mustache peculiarly adapted to
eating bean soup, up to the man of mind on whose brow is
stamped nobility. Gamblers too may here & there be seen
men whose baggage is said to be "a pack of cards, a bowie
knife & dirty shirt." This is the fashionable drinking depot
of the American part of the city. At 11 o'clock each day a
lunch is set on the table (in the spacious bar room) of meats
of all kinds, of fish, flesh & fowl and for a dime which buys
your drink you can eat what you please. Thousands daily
visit this and other similar establishments and through this
corrupt fashion the temptation to drink is fearfully great.
I think I saw over 500 persons in and about the St. Charles
Bar Room today. You can buy a lemonade if you choose &
eat as well as those who drink stronger drinks, but such are
indeed scarce. The arrangements & appointments of this hotel
are I think superior to anything I have ever seen. Far beyond any of the New York hotels. And the price & expense
is also greater. The Verandah opposite is a well kept hotel
much like the New York City hotels in appearance. It as
well as the St. Charles is built of brick and stuccoed with
plaster to give them the appearance of marble. In a cigar
store directly opposite the St. Charles is Mrs. Hamblin, the
wretched woman who killed her husband in the theatre at
Mobile & she appears to be an object of attraction even on
a/c of her murderous character. She is a coarse & vulger
looking woman & quite young. In no city in the Union is
there so much smoking and so good cigars. Cigars are sold
here as high as $80 per thousand and from a dime to half
dime each.

This magnificent establishment was built in 1835 and
fronts on three streets. Its principal front is 235 feet on
Gravier St. 195 ft. on Conuron [?] 160 ft. height from

ground to the top of general cornice 75 feet to circular colonnade under dome 96 to the top of cornice over circular colonnade 126 ft. to the top of dome 160 ft. to the top of tower on dome 185 ft. to the top of flag staff on tower 203 ft.[55]

There are in the building 353 rooms. The portico is supported by six large Corinthian columns. You ascend to the upper rooms by a spiral staircase from the saloon. The building & ground cost 600,000 dollars & the lessees of it paid 150,000 dollars to furnish it. The Verandah was finished in 1838 and cost 300,000 dollars. Altho not as fine a structure as the St. Charles yet the simplicity & chasteness of the architecture is well calculated to please the eye. It is called from the fine portico which surrounds it supported by iron pillars.

The above sketch altho' hastily drawn and coarsely executed is a very good view of the First Municipality. This is the French part of the city and is the theatre of much fashion as well as debauchery and vice. Here you see the pretty Creoles and quadroons who are so much esteemed for their beauty. Here are the masquerade balls, the gambling house, the old ruins, & the fashionable & elite many of them reside here. The custom house situated in the upper end of this municipality is a very common building and unworthy of the city. A city that has such an immense business, such an amount of shipping should have some fine public buildings and as a general rule the city is very destitute of them if you except its splendid hotels & one or two fine churches. The other buildings fronting the levee are simply ordinary stores of brick, destitute of interest or curiosity. The St. Louis Exchange seen in the distance is a well kept French hotel & a

[55] These are the figures as they appear in the manuscript; each reader is privileged to work out the computations to suit himself.

building of fine proportions. The Old Cathedral, situate back of the Parade Ground, is the object of most curiosity in this part of the city. A building whose aged walls tell us of other days long since gone by. Its style of architecture is good & the proportions of the towers & niches in good taste. Adjoining this building are the city courts on either side—and here the law is daily served out to the people in kind and quantity, as is meet, altho' not alway agreeably. You may see here almost every variety of that peculiar species of land sharks called lawyers, from the dignified and grave judges of the court to the pert law student who has hardly finished reading the titles of the books in the office. Lawyers with whiskers & without, with owl eyes & lawyers with eyes like bulls. Everything from the poor briefless attorney to the highest rank in the profession may be seen. And here too you can see all kinds of cases from the criminal case of the recorder's court to cases of importance involving millions. The probate's court, abounding with "vidders," orphans, heirs at law who are perpetuating their memory of deceased friends by lawing about the will. The Picayune say that there is a moral in this court, which shows that however wisely men may live their wills prove them little better than fools.

The criminal court is the one of most interest to a stranger, for here a casual glance will tell you much of the morals of this great city. Such varieties in crime. Such diversity of physiognomy. Broken headed Irishmen, genteel pick pockets, pock marked burly burglars. Frail women & dissipated youngsters on the highway to ruin all come up here in a heterogeneous mass to receive unasked good advice & pay the penalty due their crimes. The Merchants Exchange, a very ordinary building for such purpose, is near Canal

Street. The post office & general reading room is here and this is a great resort for business men, to compare notes, read the papers, hear gossip &c &c. Of an evening the crowd presents quite an animated scene, and altho the building & rooms are less fine yet a vast amount of business is here done & the place is thronged. The reading room is a monopoly & the charges are enormous, $10 to each individual, or to each partner of a firm. As usual a bar room & cigar shop are connected with the building.

The market is a world of itself, full of busy restless mortals and every variety & branch of trade would almost seem to be represented in and about the New Orleans market. From the cup of coffee to the highest purchases made at marketings all kinds of trade seem represented. The U. S. Mint is like all other mints, a well arranged building where all is system & gold & silver is converted into a currency with the regularity of clock work. An hour's walk through the French part of the city will convince even the most sceptical that "this is a great country." The entire municipality seems to wear more or less of a foreign air. The dress, the physiognomy, the manner of doing business is all unlike American cities and bears on its face the impress of a foreign city. And among all its diversified scenes of gaiety & sorrow of religion & vice you are continually pained by the contemplation of such giddy thoughtlessness & light hearted vice. Morality is indeed at a low ebb in many parts of this first municipality.

The Orleans Cotton Press is the finest building of the kind in the world. The ground occupied by this establishment is 632 feet in length and 308 in breadth & cost $753,558. It can store 25,000 bales and compresses annually 150,000 bales. It was burned down the week before I came to New

Orleans. The St. Mary's market is a fine building 486 feet by 42 feet, plain in its exterior and neat in its general appearance. The chief attraction as in all markets is the variety of articles exposed for sale. Poydras St. Market, which cannot be seen from the river, is another very fine market 402 feet long. The church of St. Patrick's I have described before very fully. The Presbyterian & Methodist churches are built in good proportions but are not fine buildings. The Presbyterian is of the Grecian Doric order & the Methodist of the same. Cost about $50,000 dollars each.

The St. Charles Theatre, the American Theatre & the Amphitheatre are very common buildings as are the other hotels in this part of the city. The banking houses & other public buildings are neat & plain structures, well built and in very good taste.

This elegant building occupied for the St. Louis hotel is one of the best hotels in America. It is the fashionable resort for the French portion of the population and many Americans prefer it to the St. Charles. It is conducted in much the same manner and is constantly full. The basement is occupied for stores, shops & auction rooms and you can amuse yourself well in listening to the *"harf & harf"* language of the auctioneer now crying in French and now in English. This would present a beautiful appearance were it well situated but unfortunately the streets are here very narrow and it detracts much from the appearance of the building.

This beautiful building occupies 300 feet on St. Louis St. by 120 on Royal & Charter St. It is of the Tuscan & Doric orders. The vestibule of the building is a fine room of 127 feet long and 40 feet wide. You pass through this into a beautiful rotunda which is used for business: and this is surrounded by galleries and the beauty of the whole produces a fine effect. The building includes a hotel capable of accommodating 200 persons & Exchange ball rooms with a fine painted ceiling. The basement is occupied in part by stores &c. The dome is a beauty of itself and ornamented with some elegant pencillings & fresco paintings and the effect of the light falling through the dome is very fine indeed. Altogether the attractions of this hotel are unrivalled in America and it is an exceedingly fashionable resort for pleasure seekers. The price, as of all good hotels, is 2½ per day.

The paintings in the rotunda of this house are very fine and do great credit to the artists who designed them, Canova & Pinoli, and the dreamy softness of the light as it falls on the mosaic pavement below makes it almost appear to be a scene of enchantment. The entrance to the hotel is very fine & you ascend to the different apartments by means of circular stairs. All in all none can desire a finer & more commodious hotel.

From sketch by J. Gibson.

"The church of St. Louis seen in the centre of this engraving or cathedral was commenced 1792. The architecture of this building is by no means pure, but it is not wanting in effect on that account. The lower story is of the rustic order flanked at each side of the front angles by hexagonal towers, showing below by their projecting ½ of their diameter Tuscan antae at each angle and above pilasters of plain mason work in the same style, with the antique wreaths on the frieze of the entablatures. These towers are crowned by low spires. The grand entrance to the cathedral is in the centre of the front and is a semicircular arched door with two clustered Tuscan columns on each side. This entrance is flanked by two smaller similar to the principal one. The second story of the front has the same general appearance as to the number of columns &c as the lower one but is of the Roman Doric order. Above & corresponding to the principal entrance is a circular window with niches on either side above the side doors below. On the apex of the pediment to this story rises the principal turret being in the Tuscan style & in two parts—the lower being square & 20 feet high with circular aperture on each side for letting out the sound flanked by antae. The proportions of the order were observed in the belfry which was not erected until 1824.

The front building on the right of the cathedral is of the Tuscan order in the lower story and of Ionic in the upper story. The building on the left is in all respects like the other and both are occupied by the city courts. The vegetable & meat markets here cost the city near 50,000 dollars and are very common buildings. The old convent of the Ursulines and chapel annexed to it are curiosities situated in Conde street. The convent was built in 1733 and bids fair to last many years longer. It is now used as a residence. In 1732 the population of New Orleans was only 5000 whites. In 1812 the first steamboat came to New Orleans and now she has her thousands. The city is situated on a bend on the left bank of the river forming a beautiful crescent & 105 miles from the mouth of the Mississippi. The average mortality of this place is about 4000, some years many more. The schools are very good and the Catholic schools deserve a high rank in literary character, and were it not for the dogmas of that church are to be preferred to any here. To a stranger the city is full of interest and presents a foreign appearance in many parts of the city.

INDEX

INDEX

INDEX

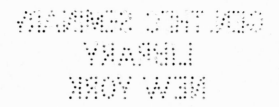